"Peace be with all of you!"

The Message & Mission of
Pope Leo XIV

Deacon Greg Kandra

Includes *Dilexi Te*,
Pope Leo's First Apostolic Exhortation

© Dicastero per la Comunicazione - Libreria Editrice Vaticana

Copyright © 2025 The Word Among Us Press

All rights reserved.

Published by The Word Among Us Press

7115 Guilford Drive, Suite 100

Frederick, Maryland 21704

wau.org

29 28 27 26 25   1 2 3 4 5

ISBN: 978-1-59325-743-9

eISBN: 978-1-59325-744-6

Design by Rose Audette

No part of this publication may be reproduced, stored in a retrieval system, or transmitted in any form or by any means—electronic, mechanical, photocopy, recording, or any other—except for brief quotations in printed reviews, without the prior permission of the author and publisher.

Contents

Preface 5

1. The Pilgrim 9
2. The Altar Boy 17
3. The Augustinian 23
4. The Missionary 31
5. The Servant 37
6. The Preacher 43

Afterword 53

Dilexi Te (On Love for the Poor) 57

Notes 117

Preface

Once the shock wore off, there was amazement. This was something none of us had ever seen before.

When the new pope appeared on the balcony of St. Peter's on May 8, 2025, history was being written, and then rewritten. It was a moment of firsts. The first North American pope. The first Augustinian pope. The first pope born in the 1950s—a Baby Boomer! Cardinal Robert Francis Prevost—the sixty-nine-year-old missionary from Chicago who had lived most of his life in Peru—stepped onto the world stage as Pope Leo XIV and jaws dropped.

And a lot of us watching at home wondered: "Okay. But who is he?"

This little book is an attempt to help answer that question.

Newspapers and magazines have told his biography breathlessly—his roots in middle America, his upbringing in a devout family, his decision to pursue religious life when still very young, all of this leading eventually to his missionary work in Peru before he was summoned to Rome and given the red hat of a cardinal in 2023.

But is there something more?

I think so.

The book you hold in your hands is not intended to be a definitive biography or deep theological study of his life. So much of that story is still being written! But in the early months of the ministry of Pope Leo XIV, a fascinating new papacy is taking shape. And his words, actions, choices, and gestures help us to see more clearly his priorities and values, and give us an opportunity to hear his own distinct voice.

It is the voice of a priest, preaching from the most powerful pulpit on earth.

It is the voice of a servant, seeking to serve not only his God, but a billion people around the world.

It is the voice of an Augustinian, devoted to a particular charism and community, following in the footsteps of the most famous convert of the early Church.

Perhaps most importantly, it is the voice of a missionary, calling the world to join him on his new global mission—one centered on Christ and built on charity, dignity, and hope. It's not radical or revolutionary; in fact, it is a mission that is both timely and timeless. But the call comes to us from a leader few people know—a figure who is altogether new, from a new generation and a new corner of the world.

It is a voice more of the world needs to hear. To facilitate that, much of this book tells his story in his own words. Since his election, he has been telling us who he is, sharing his vision for the Church and the world. Consider this book, then, a chance to take that in and prayerfully listen to what he has to say.

Ultimately, I hope this look at the life and mission of Pope Leo leads all of us not only to answer his call with renewed zeal and purpose, but also to take it up with some help from above. Put simply: I hope this little book will serve as a call to prayer.

Preface

Praying for the Holy Father is something all Catholics are urged to undertake. We hear it at every Mass in the Eucharistic Prayer (and usually in the Universal Prayer, too). To pray for the pope is to pray for his leadership, his strength, his vision, his courage. His moral leadership is unrivaled in the world; by extension, to pray for the pope is a way to pray for the world.

To that end, each chapter concludes with a short prayer for Pope Leo. It is a small way for us to join our intentions with his, bound together in a spirit of solidarity and love.

Let us pray for him as he prays for us.

When he stood before the faithful on May 8, 2025, he had one message above all that he wanted to offer the world. His first word echoed the first word of the Resurrected Christ to his apostles, as he appeared in the upper room at a moment of uncertainty, disbelief, and fear.

Our Lord knew what his friends needed to hear then. Two thousand years later, so did Pope Leo.

As we watch this historic papacy unfold, may that message fill us with joyful hope:

"Peace be with all of you!"[1]

August 28, 2025

Feast of St. Augustine

1

THE PILGRIM

"It is very important to listen to the voice of the Lord, to listen to it, in this dialogue, and to see where the Lord is calling us towards."

—Pope Leo XIV, Homily in the Crypt of St. Peter's Basilica[2]

The new pope began his ministry at the midpoint of a Jubilee Year, whose theme was announced by his predecessor: "Pilgrims of Hope." Leo is, like all of us, another pilgrim on life's journey—yet one with a distinct story to tell, of the places he's been and just where that remarkable journey began.

When he introduced himself moments after his election, Pope Leo XIV said simply, "I am an Augustinian, a son of St. Augustine."

But long before that, he was a son of Chicago, the city H. L. Menken once described as "American in every chitling and sparerib."[3] The new pope came with a unique biography and background. Not only did he grow up in the middle of the United States, but his family tree has deep and complicated roots that are Italian, Haitian, and Creole. He even has Black family ancestors in New Orleans. The leader of the universal Church has family ties that are, in every sense, universal.

Vatican Media's official biography states his beginnings simply:

> The new Bishop of Rome was born on September 14, 1955, in Chicago, Illinois, to Louis Marius Prevost, of French and Italian descent, and Mildred Martínez, of Spanish descent. He has two brothers, Louis Martín and John Joseph.[4]

But there is so much more.

Robert and his brothers grew up in a small brick house in the working-class suburb of Dolton, Illinois, about twenty miles south of Chicago. His father worked as a school superintendent and principal; his mother was a librarian at a local Catholic school. She was especially devout—a member of the choir at St. Mary of the Assumption Parish and a parish volunteer.

His family remembers that there was no doubt young Robert was destined for religious life.

A profile of the Prevost family in *Time* magazine noted:

> Robert was a regular kid, riding his bike around the streets of the south Chicago working-class suburb of Dolton by day, playing flashlight tag by night, and occasionally squeezing the glowing goo out of fireflies and wiping it on an older brother. It didn't seem odd that he occasionally set up a pretend Communion table on the ironing board and gave his family play sacraments. John confirms that even while very young, Robert had a reputation among the neighbors, with one elderly lady telling him as they played in the yard that he'd be pope one day.[5]

His curiosity about religious life led him to a minor seminary for high school, leaving home to attend St. Augustine Seminary High School in Holland, Michigan.

"It was tough; it was rigorous," Fr. Becket Franks told *Time* magazine. Fr. Franks was a year ahead of Robert Prevost at the school. Students were up at 6 a.m. They attended Mass and two other prayer services a day and had a lot of time in close quarters together.

As *Time* described it:

> Prevost, who was co-valedictorian and yearbook editor among other accolades, had a reputation for being a good person to turn to for help with homework, especially math or languages. "He was the smartest person I think we ever met," says Franks, who is now a Benedictine monk and chaplain. "He had mastered French by the middle of high school." Students were required to undertake certain extracurricular activities (Prevost was in the choir with Franks—both sing tenor—and played tennis) and to keep up their academic performance, but mostly the school's focus was how to live in community. "Everything that we went through at St. Augustine Seminary High School prepared Robert Prevost for his position," says Franks. "Not just education but dealing with people and learning patience and how to behave."[6]

After high school, young Robert Prevost left Michigan to attend Villanova, the Augustinian university in Pennsylvania. He majored in math and minored in philosophy. Through his college years, the religious call remained persistent and strong. In the fall of 1977, he took his first vows as an Augustinian.

He spent three years in formation then headed back to Chicago to continue his studies at the Catholic Theological

Union. Prevost's spiritual director at the time, Sr. Lyn Osiek, remembered her young charge as "calm and steady. . . . Those are the two words that I would say about him. It was just like nothing fazed him. He was really a person who was at peace with himself."[7]

The Augustinians are noted for their missionary work, and friends who knew and lived with Robert Prevost said he was fascinated by the idea of serving in a foreign country.

"He was very interested in what I was doing in Peru," Bishop Daniel Turley told *Time* magazine. "Of all of them, he was the most community minded."[8]

Prevost took his solemn vows in 1981 and earned his Master of Divinity in 1982. At that point, he was sent to Rome to continue his education and study canon law at the Pontifical University of Saint Thomas Aquinas, the same school where Pope John Paul II had studied. The following year, he was ordained a priest.

The experience in Rome had a powerful impact on Fr. Prevost's formation.

"When you study in Rome, you realize that the Church is really universal," said Fr. Paul Galetto, who knew Prevost when they lived at an Augustinian residence in Rome. "Many of the Augustinians who are in the United States, we just think that the American problems are the Church's problems, but there's so much more than that."[9]

For his first assignment, Fr. Prevost was sent to Peru to become personal secretary to a bishop in Chulucanas in northern Peru. "When you're a missionary, you just learn how to do everything, from electronics to auto mechanics," Prevost said years later.[10] Peru left a powerful imprint on him.

Bishop Turley explained, "As a young priest, to . . . see how beautiful it is, how poor people can be, and yet all of the goodness and the power of people when they come together, and the wonderful things that they can do if you start breaking down prejudices and division."[11]

Prevost summed it up: "The part of ministry that most shaped my life is Peru."[12]

After a decade in Peru, he returned to the United States in 1999 after being elected provincial prior of the Augustinian Province of Mother of Good Counsel in Chicago; two and a half years later, he was prior general, and he was confirmed in 2007 for a second term.

When that term was up, he returned to CTU to continue training and teaching young Augustinians. In 2014, he was tapped by Pope Francis to return to Peru as bishop of Chiclayo.

Bishop Turley told *Time*:

> "Right after he became a bishop, we had the tremendous problem of Venezuela," describing the flood of asylum seekers who poured into Peru after the Venezuelan economy began to collapse. "One of the best bishops to work with in dealing with migrants was Bishop Robert Prevost. His diocese was so well organized to take care of them."[13]

His reputation for moderate, pastoral leadership—along with a compassionate concern for the poor—grew and spread. In 2023, Pope Francis called him back to the Vatican and named him prefect of the Dicastery for Bishops and president of the Pontifical Commission for Latin America. With that came the title of archbishop. Just a few months later, in September of 2023, he was named cardinal.

Less than two years later, on May 7, 2025, Archbishop Robert Prevost—of Chicago and Chiclayo, the boy who played priest in his house by day and played flashlight tag with his friends at night—entered the Sistine Chapel for the conclave.

One day later, he left as Pope Leo XIV.

In the first weeks after his election, his friends and family members described a figure of remarkable kindness and warmth, even when he was young: "When you think about a 13-year-old boy on the South Side of Chicago . . . typically people would not immediately say, 'Oh, kind, compassionate, humble.' But those are words that you would use," childhood friend John Donaghy told *People* magazine.[14]

"For Robert," he said, "there was a constancy of how he was and how he held himself even as a 13-year-old, which is, I mean, that's the unique part of it is 13-year-olds are developing and their hormones are raging and they're defiant and they're moody and they're pushing limits. And he was almost like the calm in the adolescent storm."

"He was always kind. Never saw him have any kind of words with anybody else. And certainly no kind of physical altercations, which was a common occurrence in the south side of Chicago," he said.

Augustinian Fr. Giuseppe Caruso said humility and compassion are his hallmarks.

"He will be the pope who will take upon himself the responsibility for a Church that is traveling at different speeds, a Church that is struggling to keep up," he told the *National Catholic Reporter*.[15]

A lot of people saw something special about Robert Francis Prevost—and those who met him as a young man saw something more than just another good priest.

After getting to know Fr. Prevost many years ago, Brendan Towell, an educator who works for the Diocese of Camden, was moved to write this prophetic observation about him in *The Augustinian* just days before the 2025 conclave was about to begin:

> [When I first met Father Prevost] I was seriously discerning the possibility of entering the Order of St. Augustine and, although I ultimately discerned another path, that conversation has remained with me for years. What struck me wasn't just that he listened. It was how he listened. Despite the busyness of the week, the weight of his responsibilities, and the symbolic importance of his presence at this historic gathering, Fr. Prevost gave me his time and his attention. In a world that often rushes past the individual heart, he made mine feel seen.
>
> Looking back, and watching his continued service in the Church, ... I can't help but think: *an Augustinian would make an excellent pope.* ... As an American, he brings an intercultural fluency that's crucial for global leadership today. Yet beyond all that, he's a man who listens. He gives time to the young and the searching and sees the human person before needing to read their resume. In the imitation of Jesus, who, whether speaking with Nicodemus by night or calling Zacchaeus down from the tree, always saw the heart before the title, the person before the position.
>
> In a Church searching for both renewal and unity, what more could we ask for in a shepherd?"[16]

A Prayer on Life's Journey

Father of us all,
you directed the life and heart of Robert Francis Prevost,
calling him to serve you.
In faith and obedience, he heard your call and followed,
and now he has committed his life
to be a "servant of the servants of all" as Pope Leo XIV.
Bless him as he continues to listen to your Spirit
and follow where you lead,
drawing all of us closer to you,
in our own love for you and your Son
and in our devoted service to one another.
We pray that the life and example of your servant Leo
will inspire us.
Lord, as we journey forward,
keep our hearts always open,
our ears always attentive,
our eyes always searching for ways to serve you
by serving others.
In particular, we pray:
Watch over and protect our Holy Father Leo
on his own journey,
as he guides your one, holy, catholic
and apostolic Church.
Amen.

†

2

The Altar Boy

"In the family, faith is handed on together with life, generation after generation. It is shared like food at the family table and like the love in our hearts."
—**Pope Leo XIV, Homily for the Jubilee of Families**[17]

We've heard it said so often: a religious vocation begins in the home.

And why not? That's where life is lived, where priorities are set, where prayers are said before meals or at bedtime, and when a sense of the holy is embedded in a young and impressionable heart. It just makes sense. Parents who teach Catholic values and customs around the dinner table or in the living room or in the car on the way to soccer practice are more likely to raise children who will seriously consider a religious vocation as they grow up.

That seems to have been the case in the Prevost house. Looking at Robert Prevost's childhood, *The New York Times* described it clearly:

> All three brothers attended elementary school at the parish school. Their mother, Mildred, was the president of the St. Mary Altar and Rosary Society, and performed in plays there, according to Noelle Neis, who remembers sitting behind the family on Sunday mornings. "They were always there," Ms. Neis said, adding, "The community revolved around the church."[18]

The Catholic world got a glimpse of that in the summer of 2025, when Pope Leo spoke to hundreds of children at the Vatican who were attending an annual summer camp. *Vatican News* noted that he took questions while he was there. One of the first was from young girl who asked if he attended Mass when he was a child:

> "Of course!" he answered enthusiastically. "Always, every Sunday, with Mom and Dad." He then shared memories from his childhood in Chicago: "Around age six, I was also an altar server in my parish. Before going to school—it was a parish school—we would attend 6:30 a.m. Mass. Mom always woke us up saying, 'Let's go to Mass.'" Serving at Mass was something he truly enjoyed. "From an early age, I was taught that Jesus is always near, that he is your best friend, and Mass was a way to find that friend, to be with Jesus—even before my First Communion."[19]

> Pope Leo also recalled that back then Mass was in Latin: "We had to learn Latin for Mass, but then it changed to English for me since I was born and raised in the US." However, he emphasized, "what mattered wasn't the language of the celebration, but the experience of being with other kids serving Mass, the

friendship, and that closeness to Jesus in the Church. It was always something beautiful."[20]

The Associated Press later reported that it was the first time the Holy Father had spoken about his Catholic upbringing since he had become pope.[21] But it was more than a minor piece of papal history; it effectively opened a window into the kind of culture that had produced the first North American pontiff.

It was a place where the parish was the social and cultural hub for the community, where prayer was more than merely a practice but was also a way of life, a way of living. The Prevost house was a home where going to church—being there, taking part in activities, volunteering time and talent—was just a given. And it helped foster in young Robert a sense of youthful devotion, a feeling of "that closeness to Jesus in the Church" that would eventually lead him into religious life.

Seeds were being planted. What started with attending Mass faithfully as a child eventually blossomed into a love of the Lord and a desire to serve him at the altar—and, ultimately, in the world.

Around the same time as that meeting with children at the Vatican, Pope Leo addressed a group of seminarians who were in Rome for the Jubilee.

He told them:

The most important thing: keep your eyes fixed on Jesus (cf. *Heb* 12:2), cultivating the relationship of friendship with Him. In this regard, as the English priest Robert Hugh Benson (1871–1914) wrote after his conversion to Catholicism: "If there is anything clear in the Gospels it is this—that Jesus Christ first and foremost desires our friendship. . . . Now the consciousness of this friendship of Jesus Christ is the very secret of the saints" (*The Friendship of Christ*, Milan 2024, 17). He asks you, as Pope Francis wrote in the Encyclical *Dilexit nos*, "never to be ashamed to tell others, with all due discretion and respect, about your friendship with him. He asks that you dare to tell others how good and beautiful it is that you found him" (no. 211). Indeed, encountering Jesus saves our life and gives us the strength and the joy to communicate the Gospel to everyone.[22]

One word recurs again and again in both his remarks to the children and to the seminarians: *friendship*.

Leo doesn't see a relationship with the Lord as something formal, remote, aloof; it is intimate, familiar, comfortable, close. To be in relationship with Jesus is to be at ease. To trust. To confide. Like one friend to another.

In late July 2025, he echoed the theme of friendship with Christ in remarks to Xaverian missionaries and seminary formators at the Vatican:

> *Cultivate friendship with Jesus.* This . . . must lie at the heart of every vocation and apostolic mission. We need personally to experience the closeness of the Master; to know that we have been seen, loved and chosen by the Lord by pure grace and without merit on our part, because it is above all our own personal experience that we then exude in our ministry. Moreover, when we form others in the priestly life and, according to our specific vocation, proclaim the Gospel in mission lands, we first radiate our personal experience of friendship with Christ, which shines through in our way of living, in our attitude, in our humanity, and in how we are capable of living out healthy relationships.[23]

Pope Leo's reflections remind us of the wisdom of St. Teresa of Ávila, who famously said, "Mental prayer is nothing less than an intimate friendship, a frequent heart-to-heart conversation with Him by whom we know ourselves to be loved."[24]

But what might be called Pope Leo's "theology of friendship" is deeply rooted in Augustinian spirituality.

St. Augustine wrote in his *Confessions*:

> You only love your friend truly, after all, when you love God in your friend, either because he is in him, or in order that he may be in him. That is true love and respect. There is no true friendship unless You weld it between souls that cling together by the charity poured forth in their hearts by the Holy Spirit.[25]

In one of his sermons, the saint said:

> If the rule of friendship urges you to love human beings freely for their own sake, how much more freely is God to be loved, who bids you love other people! There can be nothing more delightful than God. I mean, in people there are always things that cause offense; still, through friendship you force yourself to put up with things that offend you in a person, for the sake of friendship. So if you ought not to break the ties of friendship with a human being just because of some things in him you have to put up with, what things should ever force you to break the ties of friendship with God? You can find nothing more delightful than God.[26]

St. Augustine understandably looms large in the life and spirituality of Pope Leo. In many ways, he helps define this pope's view of the world.

You want to know Pope Leo XIV? Begin by getting to know St. Augustine.

A Prayer for Friendship with Christ

Jesus,
in all the challenges and struggles I face,
I pray that I stay close to you all the days of my life.
May I never be afraid to turn to you in faith and in hope,
in times of desperation and fear, and help me always to
remember that you are by my side.
I pray that others will know the closeness of your friendship,
especially our Holy Father, Pope Leo.
As he walks with you, may he gain security and strength,
consolation and joy, so that all of us may see reflected in him
a man who is a beloved friend of yours.
Watch over him and help him to guide every one of us
on our own journey of faith, a journey we pray
will lead us to be with you for all eternity.
Amen.

3

The Augustinian

"As an Augustinian, having a rich community built on the ability to share with others what happens to us, to be open to others, has been one of the greatest gifts I have been given in this life."

—Cardinal Robert Prevost, interview, 2023[27]

One constant has guided Pope Leo's life from when he was very young, and it has a name: Augustine.

Robert Prevost left his Illinois home after eighth grade to study at a Michigan boys' high school named for St. Augustine, run by an order bearing the saint's name.

So it shouldn't have surprised anyone that in his first moments as pope, Leo quoted St. Augustine, who said, "With you I am a Christian, and for you I am a bishop."[28] The pope added, "In this sense, all of us can journey together toward the homeland that God has prepared for us."

Those words said so much—about the journey of life and about a familiar theme of Leo's view of the world: friendship.

James K. A. Smith, author of a new biography of St. Augustine, reflected on all this and more in *America* magazine a few days after Leo's election:

> For St. Augustine, Baptism is not an arrival, and conversion is not the end of the road; both are just the beginning of a journey with and into God's very life. . . . Every human heart, Augustine suggests, is both running from something and running toward something. We experience alienation and unsettledness in this world, but we also have a home-hunger that compels us to look, as Pope Leo put it, for a "homeland" that we've never been to before. Christ is "the Way," and to be in Christ is to be on the way. This is also why, like Pope Francis, Leo is deeply concerned with the plight of migrants and refugees, decrying "the neglect of mercy" and "appalling violations of human dignity" in his first homily.
>
> Echoing his father, Augustine, Pope Leo emphasizes that we never undertake this journey alone. The Church is a ragtag community journeying together, like Chaucer's rowdy pilgrims. So we walk together, he emphasizes over and over, "hand in hand with God and one another." [29]

That last sentence is a beautiful summation of the Augustinian charism. A website for Augustinian vocations puts it this way:

> Saint Augustine knew the support of friends and community. He wanted his brothers to "live harmoniously, with one mind and one heart, on the way to God" (*Rule*, chapter 1). He also knew the trials of family life as his mother, Monica, desperately wept and prayed for his conversion to the Catholic faith.

All of these influences helped Augustine to go within his own heart to experience the grace of God. It was a heart with just one desire: to praise God. Augustinian spirituality is deeply personal; creating intimate spaces of interior prayer. Jesus continues to ask us "What we you looking for?". Careful reflection creates the space to realize all the pursuits that fill our lives. We assert our own desire for satisfaction through human love, ideology, and ambition.

And all the heart really craves . . . is God's love.

To learn more, just spend a little time with *The Rule of St. Augustine*—a little time is all it takes, in fact, because it's very short—and you not only get a sense of the spiritual direction of the order, but also of another prevailing theme that has animated Leo's life and mission: unity.

The first page of the *Rule* declares, "Let there be among you but one heart and one soul in God," and the last words of the first chapter conclude, "Live therefore in concord and unity together, and honor Almighty God in one another, whose temples you have become."

If you want a sense of just how important that idea is to Pope Leo, all you have to do is look at his episcopal motto: *In Illo uno unum*, which means "*In the One, we are one.*"

The Vatican website explains its significance:

> The phrase is taken from Saint Augustine's *Exposition on Psalm 127*, where he explains that "although we Christians are many, in the one Christ we are one."[30]

> In a 2023 interview with Vatican News' Tiziana Campisi, then-Cardinal Robert Francis Prevost spoke about the significance of this motto: "As can be seen from my episcopal motto, unity and communion are truly part of the charism of the Order

of Saint Augustine, and also of my way of acting and thinking," he said. "I believe it is very important to promote communion in the Church, and we know well that communion, participation, and mission are the three key words of the Synod. So as an Augustinian, for me, promoting unity and communion is fundamental."

Saint Augustine's reflection on Psalm 127 highlights the theological foundation of this idea. "Christ—head and body—is one single man. And what is the body of Christ? His Church," Augustine writes. He then adds, "Although we Christians are many, in the one Christ we are one. We are many and we are one—because we are united to Him, and if our Head is in heaven, the members will follow."[31]

Gregory Grimes, a theology instructor at Villanova who first met Robert Prevost many years ago, wrote about the new pope in the pages of *Church Life Journal* and captured something about his personality—qualities that might also be considered distinctly Augustinian:

> Fr. Peter Donohue, OSA, president of Villanova, . . . has described [Robert Prevost] as "very personable . . . he enjoys being around people . . . a wonderful sense of humor . . . but he's not real effusive." He is a real human being. And I think, especially at this time in our Church, this might be one of the most important things to remember. Given the polarizations that have been happening in the ecclesial and political realms, and the tendency to demonize public figures in general (*Laudato Si'* §47), it is important to bear in mind that it is a human being who has been summoned by the Holy Spirit to a role of service (*servus servorum dei*) beyond what any of us is truly capable of.

In this, there is a tremendous opportunity to restore unity within the Church, and to heal wounds of fissure.[32]

In 2012, thirteen years before he was elected pope, then-Fr. Prevost sat down for an interview with Catholic News Service to discuss the Synod of Bishops and evangelization—and, perhaps inevitably, the conversation turned to Augustine.

What the future pope had to say reveals much about his view of the world, a picture that is coming more sharply into focus every day:

> Because of Augustine's understanding of humanity, that human experience is actually the door that leads one into discovering who God is, and then a movement that Augustine speaks of in different areas about how going into God also leads you into solidarity with other people. And that second part of living in solidarity with others is perhaps a piece of the experience that is missing nowadays. So often today in the highly individualistic society that people are growing up in, people think that my experience is the criteria: "Am I happy?" or "Am I not happy?" What that might really be is "Do I feel pleasure?" or "Don't I feel pleasure?" or "Do I feel selfish?" and if I feel OK then that's all that matters.
>
> And I think that certainly Augustine's experience says that, "Well, that isn't enough and maybe what you're calling happiness isn't authentic happiness because you're going to lose that, too." And most things that people seem to describe as 'Well, why are you happy today?' are things that are either very superficial or at best, you know, important for a short period of time but that aren't going to last forever. And Augustine gives some insight into helping people understand that having an experience of God brings you far beyond yourself and includes

that dimension of as what I would call, human solidarity, of understanding the universal brotherhood, sisterhood of men and women and that how an authentic experience of happiness has to include other people and has to include being concerned about other people and those are elements that express, I think, a very important part of the Gospel message."[33]

On August 28, 2025, Pope Leo spoke by video to the Augustinian Province of St. Thomas of Villanova. He was accepting an honor, the St. Augustine Medal, but used the occasion to reflect more on Augustinian spirituality, his vocation, and the saint who has guided most of his life.

It offers us another beautiful insight into his spirituality and his approach to leading the Church, an approach that begins with an open heart and open ears:

> Saint Augustine reminds us that before we speak, we first must listen, and as a synodal Church, we are encouraged to re-engage in the art of listening through prayer, through silence, discernment, and reflection. We have the opportunity and responsibility to listen to the Holy Spirit; to listen to each other; to listen to the voices of the poor and those on the margins whose voices need to be heard. Saint Augustine urges us to pay attention and to listen to the inner teacher, the voice that speaks from within all of us. It is within our hearts where God speaks to us.
>
> In one of his sermons, Saint Augustine encouraged his listeners: "Do not have your heart in your ears, but your ears in your heart."
>
> What do we need to do in order to practice how to listen with the ears of our heart? The world is full of noise, and our heads and

hearts can be flooded with many different kinds of messages. These messages can fuel our restlessness and steal our joy. As a community of faith, striving to build a relationship with the Lord, may we strive to filter the noise, the divisive voices in our heads and hearts, and open ourselves up to the daily invitations to get to know God and God's love better.[34]

A Prayer for Vocations

Heavenly Father,
you call us to love you, to serve you, and to help continue
your work of creation in the world.
Thank you for calling Robert Prevost to serve you
and your people as a priest, as a missionary,
and now as Pope Leo XIV.
We pray that he leads your Church with wisdom,
with love, and with joy, to fulfill your holy will
for the pilgrim Church on earth.
May he always know your consoling presence
and be uplifted during life's most difficult times:
when the journey is lonely, when the road is difficult,
and when the burden of his office may seem
too heavy to bear.
We pray, too, for all those who are being called to
serve you in a particular way: as priests, deacons,
religious, and as laypeople.
Help all of us to discern where we are meant to go,
who we are meant to become.
Inflame our hearts with love for you—love that helps us
to better hear your call.
Give us the courage to echo the "yes" of all those
who have gone before us.
And may the woman whose "yes" changed history, our
Blessed Mother, show us the path to perfect faith
and trust in you.
Amen.

†

4

THE MISSIONARY

"I still consider myself a missionary. My vocation, like that of every Christian, is to be a missionary, to proclaim the Gospel wherever one is."
—Archbishop Robert Prevost, interview with Vatican News, 2023[35]

In so many ways, Robert Prevost has always been a man on a mission. He has spent most of his life away from home—for high school, then college, then leaving the United States to become a missionary in Peru, carrying the gospel to a new country and helping make the good news live in the hearts of the people.

Now he finds himself on a mission to evangelize the world.

In many ways, he is fulfilling the mandate of Pope John Paul II, whose 1990 encyclical *Redemptoris Missio* summoned the worldwide Church to a go forth and "sow the Gospel":

> What moves me even more strongly to proclaim the urgency of missionary evangelization is the fact that it is the primary service which the Church can render to every individual and to all humanity in the modern world, a world which has experienced marvelous achievements but which seems to have lost its sense of ultimate realities and of existence itself. . . .
>
> God is opening before the Church the horizons of a humanity more fully prepared for the sowing of the gospel. I sense that the moment has come to commit all of the Church's energies to a new evangelization and to the mission *ad gentes*. No believer in Christ, no institution of the Church can avoid this supreme duty: to proclaim Christ to all peoples.[36]

That is a proclamation Robert Prevost took to heart—and he has made it central to his own vocation.

In a 2023 interview posted on The Order of St. Augustine website, Bishop Robert Prevost reflected on the mission of the Church in the twenty-first century:

> The mission of the Church has been the same for 2,000 years, when Jesus Christ said: "Go therefore and make disciples of all nations, baptizing them in the name of the Father and of the Son and of the Holy Spirit, teaching them to observe all that I have commanded you" (Mt 28:19). We have to announce the good news of the Kingdom of God at the same time that we understand what the Church is in its universal reality. This is one of the things I learned while I was prior general of the Augustinians and it has certainly been a great grounding for the role I have now. There are many different cultures, many different languages, many different circumstances around the world where the Church responds. So when we list our priorities and weigh up the challenges before us we have to be aware that the urgencies of Italy, Spain, the United States,

Peru, or China, for example, are almost certainly not the same except in one thing: the underlying challenge that Christ left to us to preach the gospel and that this is the same everywhere. The priorities of pastoral work will always be different from one place to another, but recognizing the great richness of diversity within the people of God is tremendously useful because it makes us more sensitive when it comes time to better reach out and respond to what they expect from us.[37]

Now as pope, the words "mission" and "missionary" appear often in his homilies, speeches, and messages—beginning with his first remarks to the world on May 8, 2025, his *Urbi et Orbi* blessing after his election as pope:

> Together, we must look for ways to be a missionary Church, a Church that builds bridges and encourages dialogue, a Church ever open to welcoming, like this Square with its open arms, all those who are in need of our charity, our presence, our readiness to dialogue and our love.[38]

He followed with these words, spoken in Spanish to the people he served in Peru:

> If you also allow me a brief word, a greeting to everyone and in particular to my beloved Diocese of Chiclayo, in Peru, where a faithful people has accompanied its Bishop, shared its faith and given so much, so much, to continue being a faithful Church of Jesus Christ.[39]

Like any seasoned missionary, Leo used that moment to meet people where they are—to speak their language and offer a message of heartfelt affection, gratitude, and hope. Significantly, his first words to the world were in Italian and Spanish, not his native English. A missionary, he spoke like one of those he served, and he wanted them to hear what he had to say in their native tongue.

A few days later, he returned to the theme of mission at the conclusion of his homily during his Installation Mass as pontiff:

> This is the missionary spirit that must animate us; not closing ourselves off in our small groups, nor feeling superior to the world. We are called to offer God's love to everyone, in order to achieve that unity which does not cancel out differences but values the personal history of each person and the social and religious culture of every people.
>
> Brothers and sisters, this is the hour for love! The heart of the gospel is the love of God that makes us brothers and sisters. With my predecessor Leo XIII, we can ask ourselves today: If this criterion "were to prevail in the world, would not every conflict cease and peace return?" (*Rerum Novarum*, 20).
>
> With the light and the strength of the Holy Spirit, let us build a Church founded on God's love, a sign of unity, a missionary Church that opens its arms to the world, proclaims the word, allows itself to be made "restless" by history, and becomes a leaven of harmony for humanity.
>
> Together, as one people, as brothers and sisters, let us walk towards God and love one another.[40]

One of the first major speeches after his election came in late May 2025, in remarks prepared for the Pontifical Mission Societies. Pope Leo was in his element, speaking to other missionaries, as he talked about fostering a "spirit of missionary discipleship in all the baptized":

> Our world, wounded by war, violence, and injustice, needs to hear the Gospel message of God's love and to experience the reconciling power of Christ's grace. In this sense, the Church herself, in all her members, is increasingly called

to be "a missionary Church that opens its arms to the world, proclaims the word . . . and becomes a leaven of harmony for humanity." . . .

We see the importance of fostering a spirit of missionary discipleship in all the baptized and a sense of the urgency of bringing Christ to all people. . . .

As Societies committed to sharing in the missionary mandate of the Pope and the College of Bishops, you are called to cultivate and further promote within your members the vision of the Church as the communion of believers, enlivened by the Holy Spirit, who enables us to enter into the perfect communion and harmony of the blessed Trinity. Indeed, it is in the Trinity that all things find their unity. This dimension of our Christian life and mission is close to my heart, and is reflected in the words of Saint Augustine that I chose for my episcopal service and now for my papal ministry: *In Illo uno unum*. Christ is our Savior and in him we are one, a family of God, beyond the rich variety of our languages, cultures and experiences.[41]

Undoubtedly, as this papacy continues to unfold, this missionary pope will have much more to say about our "missionary Church" and redefine for a new generation our call to evangelize and transform the world.

A Prayer for Missionaries

O God of calling and of sending,
you have called each of us to serve you
and each other in some particular way.
Help us to discern our calling with eagerness,
with surrender, and with devotion to your will,
so that we may eagerly go where you send us.
Inspire in us a burning desire to live as missionaries
in the world, whatever our calling might be,
so that we might make known to others
the good news of Jesus Christ.
Bless and protect all those who have answered your call
to go out on mission, to spread your gospel
to every corner of the world.
Strengthen their will, inflame their hearts,
and guide their steps as they walk an often uncertain
and unpredictable path.
In particular, watch over our missionary pope, Leo,
as he continues the mission he began as a young priest: to
teach, to bless, to uplift, and to walk
with those on their pilgrim journey.
May all of us take joy in the shared mission
of awakening the world to the power of your love and mercy,
and never tire of going where you want us to be.
Amen.

†

5

THE SERVANT

"I cannot feed you with ordinary bread, but this Word is your portion. I feed you with the same table that feeds me. I am your servant."

—St. Augustine, quoted on the holy card for Robert Prevost's ordination

In the sixth century, Pope Gregory the Great coined a phrase to describe the humble work of the supreme pontiff: "*servus servorum Dei*," the servant of the servants of God." To this day, that phrase appears on any papal bull that is issued.

It was with that in mind that Pope Leo spoke to the College of Cardinals two days after his election as Pope:

Beginning with Saint Peter and up to myself, his unworthy Successor, the Pope has been a humble servant of God and of his brothers and sisters, and nothing more than this. It has been clearly seen in the example of so many of my Predecessors, and most recently by Pope Francis himself, with his example of complete dedication to service and to sober simplicity of life, his abandonment to God throughout his ministry and his serene trust at the moment of his return to the Father's house. Let us take up this precious legacy and continue on the journey, inspired by the same hope that is born of faith.[42]

This has become a prevailing theme in Leo's messages. Several times in the early days of his papacy, Pope Leo has gone back to the theme of service and serving others, underscoring how central this is to the Christian life, and especially his papacy.

In his homily at the Mass of his installation as pope, he said:

I come to you as a brother, who desires to be the servant of your faith and your joy, walking with you on the path of God's love, for he wants us all to be united in one family.[43]

In his first *Regina Caeli* address, on May 11, 2025, he brought it up again, this time in regard to vocations:

Let us ask our heavenly Father to assist us in living in service to one another, each according to his or her state of life, shepherds after his own heart capable of helping one another to walk in love and truth.[44]

Unsurprisingly, this idea is deeply embedded in the heart of almost any missionary. The impulse to give, to share, to sacrifice, and to serve is intrinsic to the calling.

Long before he became pope, then-Fr. Robert Prevost reflected on this when he was prior general of the Augustinian Order.

Speaking in Rome at a convention of the friars in 2005, he delivered an address on the subject of "servant leadership"—a phrase that originated with the AT&T executive Robert Greenleaf in the 1970s. As Fr. Prevost noted:

> Greenleaf described some of the characteristics and activities of servant-leaders, providing examples which show that individual efforts, inspired by vision and a servant ethic, can make a substantial difference in the quality of society. Greenleaf said true leaders are chosen by their followers. He discussed the skills necessary to be a servant-leader; the importance of awareness, foresight and listening; and the contrasts between coercive, manipulative and persuasive power.
>
> This style of leadership is certainly Gospel-based, and in addition, there are some Augustinian insights to human experience that give a deeper appreciation for this type of leadership, a style of leadership that is needed in Augustinian communities today.[45]

To read this speech today, two decades after it was delivered, is to get some rare insight into the thinking of the man who would be pope. It also offers us a glimpse at his own thoughts on leadership, and just maybe, his own style of leading.

It's a style steeped, above all, in humility.

Across a text that runs a dozen pages, Fr. Prevost talks about St. Mark's Gospel ("Whoever wishes to be the greatest among you will be your servant"), quotes St. Augustine ("We possess authority, but only if we serve") and underscores the importance of following the example of Christ:

> A true Christian leader, a true Augustinian leader, must first and foremost be a faithful follower of Christ. And Christ has shown us the way, which is one of humility. Leading in any other way runs the grave danger of going on the wrong path —making the true goal "my ideas," "my plans," "my personal glory." But following Christ, who is "the way, the truth, and the life" means beginning by following the footsteps of the humble Christ.[46]

We also discover that the papacy was on his mind—but in a biblical way:

> Why does Simon become "Peter," the Rock? Jesus gives Peter his new name, not based upon the kind of "earthly power" that some might wish to possess in being given authority. Jesus asks, "Simon Peter, do you love me?" And after hearing Peter's response, Jesus tells him, "Feed my sheep." Once again, we return to the call of service, of being a servant of those with whom you are called to exercise "authority." Peter is given "authority" because he has learned to love as Jesus loves; because he has learned what it means to give his life in service to others. Because Peter loved, because Peter listened to Jesus, he had a sense of "vision," of the vision of Jesus and an understanding of where the recently born community, the Church, was gradually going.
>
> Any effective leader must have a sense of vision. But as Augustinians, we do not necessarily have to hold the entire vision ourselves, individually. Because of our sense of community, and of looking for the presence of the Spirit in community, we can come to identify our vision precisely in and through the community. There is an interesting image, of which I was reminded on one occasion when I was presented with a gift in Papua. The gift was a wood carving of two hunters, one standing on the shoulders of another. The leader, in turn, is not necessarily the tallest person in the group. Together, in order to see where we are going, the community lifts up one person, the leader, who is then able to see, with the help of the community, where the group ought to be moving. The leader's job then becomes to help assure that the process to get to that identified goal takes place, and in an effective manner. He knows how to promote collaboration and a true team spirit.[47]

With clarity, precision, empathy and prayerful humility, Fr. Prevost lays out the qualities of a true "servant leader" and links all that to Augustine's own thoughts on leadership. Here, he explains, is what the saint had to say about the ordination of a bishop:

> The man, you see, who presides over the people out first of all to understand that he is the servant of many masters. And let him not disdain this role; let him not, I repeat, disdain to be the servant of many people, because the Lord of lords did not disdain to serve us. You will remember that from the dregs of the flesh a certain appetite for superiority, for being top dog, had crept in among the disciples of our Lord Jesus Christ, our apostles, and the fumes of conceit had begun to obscure their vision. As we can read in the gospel, in fact, there arose a dispute among them, about which of them was to be the greatest (Lk 9:46). The Lord, however, present as the doctor, lanced this tumor of theirs. When he saw what vice this dispute arose from, he said to them, placing small children in front of himself, Unless a person becomes like this child, he shall not enter the kingdom of heaven. What he was drawing their attention to in the child was humility.[48]

It becomes increasingly clear that his concern with and attention to humility is one of the defining qualities of this pope—and it something he is seeking to bring into the wider Church and, even, the world.

A Prayer for the Servant

Creator God,
you made us to know you,
to love you, and to serve you.
May we always remain close to you
and remember that in serving others, we serve you,
for everyone is made in your image and likeness.
We pray for all who have devoted their lives
to serving you, and we hold in our hearts
your devoted servant, Pope Leo XIV.
We give thanks for his dedication, his commitment,
his sacrifice, and pray that he may continue
to serve you and your people
with devotion, with compassion, and with joy.
We pray that he will show us through his leadership
how to serve, and guide us to more faithfully seek ways
to give ourselves to you by giving more
of ourselves to others.
Amen.

✝

6

THE PREACHER

*"There is a need for renewed zeal in the proclamation
and transmission of faith. It is a question of placing
Jesus Christ at the center, . . . helping people to live
out a personal relationship with Him, to discover the
joy of the Gospel."*

—**Pope Leo XIV, Speech to the Italian
Episcopal Conference**[49]

What do you preach about when you have the largest pulpit in the world? For Pope Leo, the first months of his papacy have revealed a preacher who is using that pulpit to speak about concerns that are close to his heart—and that touch all of us in one way or another.

As diverse and varied as his topics and audiences may be, many of his homilies and speeches have focused on a few recurring themes. Three in particular leap out:

Peace. Unity. Hope.

PEACE

As Pope Leo marked a milestone as pontiff, the website *Aleteia* noted that he mentioned peace one hundred times during his first one hundred days:

> [Peace] was, after all, the very first word and wish he expressed as Peter.
>
> Peace is the mission of the Church—She must proclaim this peace, as the Risen Christ did.
>
> He affirmed this to Catholic digital missionaries on July 29:
>
>> This is the mission of the Church: to proclaim peace to the world! The peace that comes from the Lord, who conquered death, brings us God's forgiveness, gives us the life of the Father, and shows us the way of Love!
>
> The Holy Father has reflected that to be channels of this peace, we must ourselves be at peace, deep down.
>
> "Only a peaceful heart can spread peace in the family, society, and international relations," said Leo XIV at the end of Pentecost Mass, celebrated on June 8, 2025.
>
> To be peacemakers was the first exhortation he made to journalists, just four days after his election, saying that the beatitude "Blessed are the peacemakers" is "particularly relevant" to those in this field.
>
> He urged them to strive for a kind of communication that "never separates the search for truth from the love with which we must humbly seek it."
>
> He told them:
>
>> Peace begins with each one of us: in the way we look at others, listen to others and speak about others. In this sense, the way we communicate is of fundamental importance: We must say "no" to the war of words and images, we must reject the paradigm of war.[50]

In a world fraught with conflict, division, polarization, and war, is it any wonder that he continually preaches peace? In the early months of his papacy, he has also taken pains to encourage dialogue and listening—two tools that can only help to facilitate peace.

On May 11, 2025, preaching in the crypt of St. Peter's, he said in his homily:

> How important it is to listen! Jesus says, "My sheep listen to my voice." And I think it is important for all of us to learn how to listen more, to enter into dialogue. First and foremost, with the Lord: always listen to the Word of God. Then also listen to others, to know how to build bridges, to know how to listen without judging, not closing the doors thinking that we have all the truth and no-one else can tell us anything. It is very important to listen to the voice of the Lord, to listen to it, in this dialogue, and to see where the Lord is calling us towards.[51]

Speaking to the Italian bishops in June of 2025, he expressed this wish for the local church:

> May every community become a "house of peace," where one learns how to defuse hostility through dialogue, where justice is practiced and forgiveness is cherished. Peace is not a spiritual utopia: it is a humble path, made up of daily gestures that interweave patience and courage, listening and action, and which demands today, more than ever, our vigilant and generative presence....
>
> I particularly recommend cultivating a culture of dialogue. It is good for all ecclesial realities—parishes, associations and movements—to be spaces of intergenerational listening, of comparison with different worlds, of caring about words and relationships. Because only where there is listening can

communion be born, and only where there is communion does truth become credible. I encourage you to continue on this path!

UNITY

The pope's very title, *Pontifex Maximus*, means "great bridge-builder." Pope Leo has begun his ministry as that pontiff seeking to span differences and speak fervently and often about unity.

Unity is a preeminent theme among Augustinians. A popular commentary accompanying *The Rule of St. Augustine*, attributed to Hugh of St. Victor, offers this thought:

> This is the end for which we are gathered in one: namely, that we may have one spirit and one soul in the service of God. And therefore the command is that we dwell together in the same house and have but one soul and one heart in God. . . .
>
> We are a number of individuals under one roof, with different ways of acting, different hearts, different wills: all which one intention and one love of God must weld together in unity.[52]

During the homily of his Mass of installation, Pope Leo expressed that idea this way:

> Brothers and sisters, I would like that our first great desire be for *a united Church, a sign of unity and communion, which becomes a leaven for a reconciled world.*
>
> In this our time, we still see too much discord, too many wounds caused by hatred, violence, prejudice, the fear of difference, and an economic paradigm that exploits the Earth's resources and marginalizes the poorest. For our part, we want to be a small leaven of unity, communion and fraternity within the world. We want to say to the world, with humility and joy: Look to Christ! Come closer to him! Welcome his word that enlightens

and consoles! Listen to his offer of love and become his one family: *in the one Christ, we are one.* This is the path to follow together, among ourselves but also with our sister Christian churches, with those who follow other religious paths, with those who are searching for God, with all women and men of good will, in order to build a new world where peace reigns!

This is the missionary spirit that must animate us; not closing ourselves off in our small groups, nor feeling superior to the world. We are called to offer God's love to everyone, in order to achieve that unity which does not cancel out differences but values the personal history of each person and the social and religious culture of every people.[53]

A few weeks later, speaking to a gathering of lay associations, ecclesial movements, and new communities, he underscored unity once again:

First of all, [you must be] a *leaven of unity.* All of you constantly experience the spiritual communion that unites you. It is the communion that the Holy Spirit brings about in the Church. It is a unity that has its foundation in Christ, who draws us to himself and thus unites us with one another. Saint Paulinus of Nola once wrote in a letter to Saint Augustine: "We have one Head, one grace that fills us, we live on one Bread, we walk on one path and we live in the same house.... We are one, in both the spirit and the body of the Lord. If we separate ourselves from that One, we become nothing" (Ep. 30, 2).

Seek to spread everywhere this unity that you yourselves experience in your groups and communities, always in communion with the Church's pastors and in solidarity with other ecclesial realities. Draw close to all those whom you meet, so that your charisms may ever be at the service of the unity of the

Church, and be "a leaven of unity, communion, and fraternity" (cf. Homily, 18 May 2025) in our world, so torn by discord and violence.[54]

HOPE

Leo has begun his papacy by continuing the theme that his predecessor proclaimed for the Jubilee, refocusing hearts and minds on one distinct message: hope.

As Pope Francis put it in the bull introducing the Holy Year:

> Everyone knows what it is to hope. In the heart of each person, hope dwells as the desire and expectation of good things to come, despite our not knowing what the future may bring. Even so, uncertainty about the future may at times give rise to conflicting feelings, ranging from confident trust to apprehensiveness, from serenity to anxiety, from firm conviction to hesitation and doubt. Often we come across people who are discouraged, pessimistic and cynical about the future, as if nothing could possibly bring them happiness. For all of us, may the Jubilee be an opportunity to be renewed in hope. God's word helps us find reasons for that hope.[55]

Pope Leo has sought to remind his flock again and again how vital it is, quite simply, to *hope*.

A few weeks into his papacy, he made his first direct speech to an audience in the United States: he recorded a video message for young people gathered at his home turf in Chicago's White Sox stadium:

> I'd like to say that you are the promise of hope for so many of us. The world looks to you as you look around yourselves and say: we need you, we want you to come together to share with us in this common mission, as Church and in society, of

announcing a message of true hope and of promoting peace, promoting harmony, among all peoples. . . .

"Hope does not disappoint," Saint Paul tells us in his letter to the Romans (5:5). When I see each and every one of you, when I see how people gather together to celebrate their faith, I discover myself how much hope there is in the world.[56]

After imparting that message to the young, he shared it as well with the old, offering these words in a message for the World Day for Grandparents and the Elderly:

The Jubilee we are now celebrating helps us to realize that hope is a constant source of joy, whatever our age. When that hope has also been tempered by fire over the course of a long life, it proves a source of deep happiness. . . .

May we always praise God for his goodness, cultivate unity with our loved ones, open our hearts to those who are far away and, in particular, to all those in need. In this way, we will be signs of hope, whatever our age.[57]

Tying his preaching to the Holy Year, Leo also delivered a series of talks on the subject of hope as the catechesis of his General Audience—even finding a message of hope in moments such as Christ's agony in the Garden of Gethsemane:

The way that Jesus exercised his freedom in the face of death teaches us not to fear suffering, but to persevere in confident trust in God's providential care. May our lives always be marked by this hope, born of the knowledge that if we surrender to God's will and freely give our lives in love for others, the Father's grace will sustain us in every trial and enable us to bear abundant fruit for the salvation of our brothers and sisters.[58]

The result of all this? Pope Leo stands today as a figure of quiet serenity and optimism—declaring peace, unity and hope in a time battered by war, conflict, and despair. The words Pope Benedict XVI used to describe St. Augustine in *Spe Salvi* bear remembering. A "son of Augustine" is now trying to continue the work his spiritual father began:

> Amid the serious difficulties facing the Roman Empire—and also posing a serious threat to Roman Africa, which was actually destroyed at the end of Augustine's life—this was what he set out to do: to transmit hope, the hope which came to him from faith and which, in complete contrast with his introverted temperament, enabled him to take part decisively and with all his strength in the task of building up the city.[59]

A Prayer for Preachers

Lord,
I pray for all who seek to spread your word,
as teachers and writers, as catechists and preachers.
I pray especially for the most important voice
proclaiming your word, our Holy Father, Pope Leo XIV.
Send your Holy Spirit to enkindle in him
the fire of your love, so that the flame of faith
may spread from heart to heart, soul to soul.
I pray that more will come to believe and be changed,
and that they will also come to know
the good news of your Son through your servant Leo,
your missionary to the global Church.
Help all of us to listen more closely
and love more completely,
so that we may live your word in the world.
I pray that when my pilgrim journey
has come to an end,
I may be welcomed into the dwelling place
you have prepared.
Amen.

✝

Afterword

On the morning of September 30, 2023, Pope Francis installed 21 new cardinals—including the bishop of Chiclayo, Peru, who also happened to be the prefect of the Dicastery for Bishops, Robert Prevost, OSA. Members of the Augustinian order were understandably thrilled. They took this opportunity to videotape an extensive interview with the new cardinal.[60] It was a beautiful autumn day in Rome, and the interview was conducted outside, with St. Peter's Basilica forming the perfect backdrop.

During the interview, the new cardinal shared his thoughts about a variety of topics. His comments all this time later resonate differently. They carry more weight.

Since he was in charge of the department that helps select bishops, the new Cardinal Prevost was asked what makes a good bishop. His answer was simple, direct, and down-to-earth.

"To be a good shepherd," he replied, "means to be able to walk side-by-side with the people of God and to live close to them, not to be isolated. Pope Francis has made this very clear on numerous occasions. He does not want bishops who live in palaces. He wants bishops who live in relationship with God, with their brother bishops, with priests, and especially with the people of God in a way that reflects the compassion and love of

Christ, creating community, learning to live what it means to be part of the Church in an integral way that necessitates a lot of listening and dialogue.... If I had to point out one trait above all others, it is that he must proclaim Jesus Christ and live the faith so that the faithful see in his witness an incentive to them to want to be an ever more active part of the Church that Jesus Christ himself founded. In just a few words: to help people come to know Christ through the gift of faith."

Elsewhere in the interview, he talked about his love of tennis—"I consider myself quite the amateur tennis player," he joked—and the value of his friendships in the community and in his faith. "The gift of friendship brings us back to Jesus himself," he said. "To have the ability to develop authentic friendships in life is beautiful. Without a doubt, friendship is one of the most wonderful gifts that God has given us."

In one revealing moment, he also spoke about relocating to Rome in his new job as head of Vatican Discastery. How did he feel about that?

"I have always done what I have been asked to do," he said, "whether in the Order or in the Church."

He spoke of missing the people of Peru and how much he enjoyed his time there. But he was also philosophical and forward-looking—and willing to go wherever God wanted.

"Every day," he replied, "I say to myself: 'Lord, all this is in your hands. Give me the grace I need to bring this task to a successful conclusion. And as I have tried to do throughout my religious life, I said yes, go ahead with the great adventure of being a follower of Christ."

The most important chapter of his adventure is just beginning.

A Prayer for Pope Leo

Heavenly Father,
look with love upon your servant Leo,
as he undertakes the great and humbling work
of leading your Church.
Hear our prayers at this moment:
protect him, uplift him, strengthen him;
continue to inflame his heart with love for your word
and compassion for your children.
May he know your friendship when he is most in need,
and never doubt that you are near
as he walks his pilgrim journey on a mission to serve
and to lead, to listen and to preach,
moved by an unwavering love
for you and your Son.
Our broken world cries out:
in a time of war, help him be a voice for peace;
in a time of division, help him be a force for unity;
in an age of despair, help him to fill our hearts with hope.
Grant him the grace to lead always with love,
so that through him we may draw ever closer to you.
We ask this through our Lord Jesus Christ, your Son,
who lives and reigns with you and the Holy Spirit,
God forever and ever.
Amen.

✝

Apostolic Exhortation
Dilexi Te
(On Love for the Poor)

1. "I have loved you" (*Rev* 3:9). The Lord speaks these words to a Christian community that, unlike some others, had no influence or resources, and was treated instead with violence and contempt: "You have but little power... I will make them come and bow down before your feet" (*Rev* 3:8-9). This text reminds us of the words of the canticle of Mary: "He has cast down the mighty from their thrones, and lifted up the lowly; he has filled the hungry with good things, and sent the rich away empty" (*Lk* 1:52-53).

2. This declaration of love, taken from the Book of Revelation, reflects the inexhaustible mystery that Pope Francis reflected upon in the Encyclical *Dilexit Nos* on the human and divine love of the heart of Jesus Christ. There we saw how Jesus identified himself "with the lowest ranks of society" and how, with his love poured out to the end, he confirms the dignity of every human being, especially when "they are weak, scorned, or suffering."[61] As we contemplate Christ's love, "we too are inspired to be more attentive to the sufferings and needs of others, and confirmed in our efforts to share in his work of liberation as instruments for the spread of his love."[62]

3. For this reason, in continuity with the Encyclical *Dilexit Nos*, Pope Francis was preparing in the last months of his life an Apostolic Exhortation on the Church's care for the poor, to which he gave the title *Dilexi Te*, as if Christ speaks those words to each of them, saying: "You have but little power," yet "I have loved you" (*Rev* 3:9). I am happy to make this document my own — adding some reflections — and to issue it at the beginning of my own pontificate, since I share the desire of my beloved predecessor that all Christians come to appreciate the close connection between Christ's love and his summons to care for the poor. I too consider it essential to insist on this path to holiness, for "in this call to recognize him in the poor and the suffering, we see revealed the very heart of Christ, his deepest feelings and choices, which every saint seeks to imitate."[63]

CHAPTER ONE

A FEW ESSENTIAL WORDS

4. Jesus' disciples criticized the woman who poured costly perfumed oil on his head. They said: "Why this waste? For this ointment could have been sold for a large sum, and the money given to the poor." However, the Lord said to them in response: "You always have the poor with you, but you will not always have me" (*Mt* 26:8-9,11). That woman saw in Jesus the lowly and suffering Messiah on whom she could pour out all her love. What comfort that anointing must have brought to the very head that within a few days would be pierced by thorns! It was a small gesture, of course, but those who suffer know how great even a small gesture of affection can be, and how much relief it can bring. Jesus understood this and told the disciples that the memory of her gesture would endure: "Wherever this good news is proclaimed in the whole world, what she has done will be told in remembrance of her" (*Mt* 26:13). The simplicity of that woman's gesture speaks volumes. No sign of affection, even the smallest, will ever be forgotten, especially if it is shown to those who are suffering, lonely or in need, as was the Lord at that time.

5. Love for the Lord, then, is one with love for the poor. The same Jesus who tells us, "The poor you will always have with you" (*Mt* 26:11), also promises the disciples: "I am with you always" (*Mt* 28:20). We likewise think of his saying: "Just as you did it to one of the least of these brothers and sisters of mine, you did it to me" (*Mt* 25:40). This is not a matter of mere human kindness but a revelation: contact with those who are lowly and powerless is a fundamental way of encountering the Lord of history. In the poor, he continues to speak to us.

SAINT FRANCIS

6. Pope Francis, explaining his choice of that name, related how, after his election, a Cardinal friend of his embraced him, kissed him and told him: "Do not forget the poor!"[64] It is the same appeal that the leaders of the Church made to Saint Paul when he went up to Jerusalem to confirm his mission (cf. *Gal* 2:1-10). Years later, the Apostle could still reaffirm that this was "actually what I was eager to do" (*Gal* 2:10). Care for the poor was also a great concern of Saint Francis of Assisi: in the person of a leper, Christ himself embraced Francis and changed his life. Even today, Saint Francis, as the Poor Man of Assisi, continues to inspire us by his outstanding example.

7. Eight centuries ago, Saint Francis prompted an evangelical renewal in the Christians and society of his time. Wealthy and self-confident, the young Francis was taken aback and converted by his direct contact with the poor and outcast of society. The story of his life continues to appeal to the minds and hearts of believers, and many non-believers as well. It "changed history."[65] A further step on the same path was taken by the Second Vatican Council, as Saint Paul VI pointed out when he said that "the ancient parable of the Samaritan served as the model for the Council's spirituality."[66] I am convinced that the preferential choice for the poor is a source of extraordinary renewal both for the Church and for society, if we can only set ourselves free of our self-centeredness and open our ears to their cry.

THE CRY OF THE POOR

8. The passage of Sacred Scripture in which God reveals himself to Moses in the burning bush can serve as a constant starting-point for this effort. There he says: "I have observed the misery of my people who are in Egypt; I have heard their cry on account of their taskmasters. Indeed, I know their sufferings, and I have come down to deliver them... So come, I will send you" (*Ex* 3:7-8,10).[67] God thus shows his concern for the needs of the poor: "When the Israelites cried out to the Lord, he raised up for them a deliverer" (*Judg* 3:15). In hearing the cry of the poor, we are asked to enter into the heart of God, who is always concerned for the needs of his children, especially those in greatest need. If we remain unresponsive to that cry, the poor might well cry out to the Lord against us, and we would incur guilt (cf. *Deut* 15:9) and turn away from the very heart of God.

9. The condition of the poor is a cry that, throughout human history, constantly challenges our lives, societies, political and economic systems, and, not least, the Church. On the wounded faces of the poor, we see the suffering of the innocent and, therefore, the suffering of Christ himself. At the same time, we should perhaps speak more correctly of the many faces of the poor and of poverty, since it is a multifaceted phenomenon. In fact, there are many forms of poverty: the poverty of those who lack material means of subsistence, the poverty of those who are socially marginalized and lack the means to give voice to their dignity and abilities, moral and spiritual poverty, cultural poverty, the poverty of those who find themselves in a condition of personal or social weakness or fragility, the poverty of those who have no rights, no space, no freedom.

10. In this sense, it can be said that the commitment to the poor and to removing the social and structural causes of poverty has gained importance in recent decades, but it remains insufficient. This is also the case because our societies often favor criteria for orienting life and politics that are marked by numerous inequalities. As a result, the old forms of poverty that we have become aware of and are trying to combat are being joined by new ones, sometimes more subtle and dangerous. From this point of view, it is to be welcomed that the United Nations has made the eradication of poverty one of its Millennium Goals.

11. A concrete commitment to the poor must also be accompanied by a change in mentality that can have an impact at the cultural level. In fact, the illusion of happiness derived from a comfortable life pushes many people towards a vision of life centered on the accumulation of wealth and social success at all costs, even at the expense of others and by taking advantage of unjust social ideals and political-economic systems that favor the strongest. Thus, in a world where the poor are increasingly numerous, we paradoxically see the growth of a wealthy elite, living in a bubble of comfort and luxury, almost in another world compared to ordinary people. This means that a culture still persists—sometimes well disguised—that discards others without even realizing it and tolerates with indifference that millions of people die of hunger or survive in conditions unfit for human beings. A few years ago, the photo of a lifeless child lying on a Mediterranean beach caused an uproar; unfortunately, apart from some momentary outcry, similar events are becoming increasingly irrelevant and seen as marginal news items.

12. We must not let our guard down when it comes to poverty. We should be particularly concerned about the serious conditions in which many people find themselves due to lack of food and water. In wealthy countries too, the growing numbers of the poor are equally a source of concern. In Europe, more and more families find themselves unable to make it to the end of the month. In general, we are witnessing an increase in different kinds of poverty, which is no longer a single, uniform reality but now involves multiple forms of economic and social impoverishment, reflecting the spread of inequality even in largely affluent contexts. Let us not forget that "doubly poor are those women who endure situations of exclusion, mistreatment and violence, since they are frequently less able to defend their rights. Even so, we constantly witness among them impressive examples of daily heroism in defending and protecting their vulnerable families."[68] While significant changes are under way in some countries, "the organization of societies worldwide is still far from reflecting clearly that women possess the same dignity and identical rights as men. We say one thing with our words, but our decisions and reality tell another story,"[69] especially if we consider the numbers of women who are in fact destitute.

Ideological Prejudices

13. Looking beyond the data—which is sometimes "interpreted" to convince us that the situation of the poor is not so serious—the overall reality is quite evident: "Some economic rules have proved effective for growth, but not for integral human development. Wealth has increased, but together with inequality, with the result that 'new forms of poverty are emerging.' The claim that the modern world has reduced poverty is made by measuring poverty with criteria from the past that do not correspond to present-day realities. In other times, for example, lack of access to electric energy was not considered a sign of poverty, nor was it a source of hardship. Poverty must always be understood and gauged in the context of the actual opportunities available in each concrete historical period."[70] Looking beyond specific situations and contexts, however, a 1984 document of the European Community declared that "'the poor' shall be taken to mean persons, families and groups of persons whose resources (material, cultural and social) are so limited as to exclude them from the minimum acceptable way of life in the Member States in which they live."[71] Yet if we acknowledge that all human beings have the same dignity, independent of their place of birth, the immense differences existing between countries and regions must not be ignored.

14. The poor are not there by chance or by blind and cruel fate. Nor, for most of them, is poverty a choice. Yet, there are those who still presume to make this claim, thus revealing their own blindness and cruelty. Of course, among the poor there are also those who do not want to work, perhaps because their ancestors, who worked all their lives, died poor. However, there are so many others—men and women—who nonetheless work from dawn to dusk, perhaps collecting scraps or the like, even though they know that their hard work will only help them to scrape by, but never really improve their lives. Nor can it be said that most of the poor are such because they do not "deserve" otherwise, as maintained by that specious view of meritocracy that sees only the successful as "deserving."

15. Christians too, on a number of occasions, have succumbed to attitudes shaped by secular ideologies or political and economic approaches that lead to gross generalizations and mistaken conclusions. The fact that some dismiss or ridicule charitable works, as if they were an obsession on the part of a few and not the burning heart of the Church's mission, convinces me of the need to go back and re-read the Gospel, lest we risk replacing it with the wisdom of this world. The poor cannot be neglected if we are to remain within the great current of the Church's life that has its source in the Gospel and bears fruit in every time and place.

CHAPTER TWO

GOD CHOOSES THE POOR

THE CHOICE OF THE POOR

16. God is merciful love, and his plan of love, which unfolds and is fulfilled in history, is above all his descent and coming among us to free us from slavery, fear, sin and the power of death. Addressing their human condition with a merciful gaze and a heart full of love, he turned to his creatures and thus took care of their poverty. Precisely in order to share the limitations and fragility of our human nature, he himself became poor and was born in the flesh like us. We came to know him in the smallness of a child laid in a manger and in the extreme humiliation of the cross, where he shared our radical poverty, which is death. It is easy to understand, then, why we can also speak theologically of a preferential option on the part of God for the poor, an expression that arose in the context of the Latin American continent and in particular in the Puebla Assembly, but which has been well integrated into subsequent teachings of the Church.[72] This "preference" never indicates exclusivity or discrimination towards other groups, which would be impossible for God. It is meant to emphasize God's actions, which are moved by compassion toward the poverty and weakness of all humanity. Wanting to inaugurate a kingdom of justice, fraternity and solidarity, God has a special place in his heart for those who are discriminated against and oppressed, and he asks us, his Church, to make a decisive and radical choice in favor of the weakest.

17. It is in this perspective that we can understand the numerous pages of the Old Testament in which God is presented as the friend and liberator of the poor, the one who hears the cry of the poor and intervenes to free them (cf. *Ps* 34:7). God, the refuge of the poor, denounces through the prophets—we recall in particular Amos and Isaiah—the injustices committed against the weakest, and exhorts Israel to renew its worship from within, because one cannot pray and offer sacrifice while oppressing the weakest and poorest. From the beginning of Scripture, God's love is vividly demonstrated by his protection of the weak and the poor, to the extent that he can be said to have a particular fondness for them. "God's heart has a special place for the poor... The entire history of our redemption is marked by the presence of the poor."[73]

JESUS, THE POOR MESSIAH

18. The Old Testament history of God's preferential love for the poor and his readiness to hear their cry—to which I have briefly alluded—comes to fulfillment in Jesus of Nazareth.[74] By his Incarnation, he "emptied himself, taking the form of a slave, being born in human likeness" (*Phil* 2:7), and in that form he brought us salvation. His was a radical poverty, grounded in his mission to reveal fully God's love for us (cf. *Jn* 1:18; *1 Jn* 4:9). As Saint Paul puts it in his customarily brief but striking manner: "You know well the grace of our Lord Jesus Christ, that though he was rich, yet for your sakes he became poor, so that by his poverty you might become rich" (*2 Cor* 8:9).

19. The Gospel shows us that poverty marked every aspect of Jesus' life. From the moment he entered the world, Jesus knew the bitter experience of rejection. The Evangelist Luke tells how Joseph and Mary, who was about to give birth, arrived in Bethlehem, and then adds, poignantly, that "there was no place for them in the inn" (*Lk* 2:7). Jesus was born in humble surroundings and laid in a manger; then, to save him from being killed, they fled to Egypt (cf. *Mt* 2:13-15). At the dawn of his public ministry, after announcing in the synagogue of Nazareth that the year of grace which would bring joy to the poor was fulfilled in him, he was driven out of town (cf. *Lk* 4:14-30). He died as an outcast, led out of Jerusalem to be crucified (cf. *Mk* 15:22). Indeed, that is how Jesus' poverty is best described: he experienced the same exclusion that is the lot of the poor, the outcast of society. Jesus is a manifestation of this *privilegium pauperum*. He presented himself to the world not only as a poor Messiah, but also as the Messiah of and for the poor.

20. There are some clues about Jesus' social status. First of all, he worked as a craftsman or carpenter, *téktōn* (cf. *Mk* 6:3). These were people who earned their living by manual labor. Not owning land, they were considered inferior to farmers. When the baby Jesus was presented in the Temple by Joseph and Mary, his parents offered a pair of turtledoves or pigeons (cf. *Lk* 2:22-24), which according to the prescriptions of the Book of Leviticus (cf. 12:8) was the offering of the poor. A fairly significant episode in the Gospel tells us how Jesus, together with his disciples, gathered heads of grain to eat as they passed through the fields (cf. *Mk* 2:23-28). Only the poor were allowed to do this gleaning in the fields. Moreover, Jesus says of himself: "Foxes have holes, and birds of the air have nests; but the Son of Man has nowhere to lay his head" (*Mt* 8:20; *Lk* 9:58). He is, in fact, an itinerant teacher, whose poverty and precariousness are signs of his bond with the Father. They are also conditions for those who wish to follow him on the path of discipleship. In this way, the renunciation of goods, riches and worldly securities becomes a visible sign of entrusting oneself to God and his providence.

21. At the beginning of his public ministry, Jesus appeared in the synagogue of Nazareth reading the scroll of the prophet Isaiah and applying the prophet's words to himself: "The Spirit of the Lord is upon me, because he has anointed me to bring good news to the poor" (*Lk* 4:18; cf. *Is* 61:1). He thus reveals himself as the One who, in the here and now of history, comes to bring about God's loving closeness, which is above all a work of liberation for those who are prisoners of evil, and for the weak and the poor. The signs that accompany Jesus' preaching are manifestations of the love and compassion with which God looks upon the sick, the poor and sinners who, because of their condition, were marginalized by society and even people of faith. He opens the eyes of the blind, heals lepers, raises the dead and proclaims the good news to the poor: God is near, God loves you (cf. *Lk* 7:22). This explains why he proclaims: "Blessed are you poor, for yours is the kingdom of God" (*Lk* 6:20). God shows a preference for the poor: the Lord's words of hope and liberation are addressed first of all to them. Therefore, even in their poverty or weakness, no one should feel abandoned. And the Church, if she wants to be Christ's Church, must be a Church of the Beatitudes, one that makes room for the little ones and walks poor with the poor, a place where the poor have a privileged place (cf. *Jas* 2:2-4).

22. In that time, the needy and the sick, lacking the necessities of life, frequently found themselves forced to beg. They thus bore the added burden of social shame, due to the belief that sickness and poverty were somehow linked to personal sin. Jesus firmly countered this mentality by insisting that God "makes his sun rise on the evil and on the good, and sends rain on the righteous and on the unrighteous" (*Mt* 5:45). Indeed, he completely overturned that notion, as we see from the ending of the parable of the rich man and Lazarus: "Child, remember that during your lifetime you received your good things, and Lazarus in like manner evil things; but now he is comforted here, and you are in agony" (*Lk* 16:25).

23. It becomes clear, then, that "our faith in Christ, who became poor, and was always close to the poor and the outcast, is the basis of our concern for the integral development of society's most neglected members."[75] I often wonder, even though the teaching of Sacred Scripture is so clear about the poor, why many people continue to think that they can safely disregard the poor. For the moment, though, let us pursue our reflection on what the Scriptures have to tell us about our relationship with the poor and their essential place in the people of God.

MERCY TOWARDS THE POOR IN THE BIBLE

24. The Apostle John writes: "Those who do not love a brother or sister whom they have seen, cannot love God whom they have not seen" (*1 Jn* 4:20). Similarly, in his reply to the scribe's question, Jesus quotes the two ancient commandments: "You shall love the Lord your God with all your heart, and with all your soul, and with all your might" (*Deut* 6:5), and "You shall love your neighbor as yourself" (*Lev* 19:18), uniting them in a single commandment. The Evangelist Mark reports Jesus' response in these terms: "The first is, 'Hear, O Israel: the Lord our God, the Lord is one; you shall love the Lord your God with all your heart, and with all your soul, and with all your mind, and with all your strength.' The second is this, 'You shall love your neighbor as yourself.' There is no other commandment greater than these" (12:29-31).

25. The passage from the Book of Leviticus teaches love for one's neighbor, while other texts call for respect—if not also love—even for one's enemy: "When you come upon your enemy's ox or donkey going astray, you shall bring it back. When you see the donkey of one who hates you lying under its burden and you would hold back from setting it free, you must help to set it free" (*Ex* 23:4-5). Here the intrinsic value of respect for others is expressly stated: anyone in need, even an enemy, always deserves our assistance.

26. Jesus' teaching on the primacy of love for God is clearly complemented by his insistence that one cannot love God without extending one's love to the poor. Love for our neighbor is tangible proof of the authenticity of our love for God, as the Apostle John attests: "No one has ever seen God; if we love one another, God lives in us, and his love is perfected in us... God is love, and those who abide in love abide in God, and God abides in them" (*1 Jn* 4:12,16). The two loves are distinct yet inseparable. Even in cases where there is no explicit reference to God, the Lord himself teaches that every act of love for one's neighbor is in some way a reflection of divine charity: "Truly I tell you, just as you did it to one of the least of these my brethren, you did it to me" (*Mt* 25:40).

27. For this reason, works of mercy are recommended as a sign of the authenticity of worship, which, while giving praise to God, has the task of opening us to the transformation that the Spirit can bring about in us, so that we may all become an image of Christ and his mercy towards the weakest. In this sense, our relationship with the Lord, expressed in worship, also aims to free us from the risk of living our relationships according to a logic of calculation and self-interest. We are instead open to the gratuitousness that surrounds those who love one another and, therefore, share everything in common. In this regard, Jesus advises: "When you give a dinner or a banquet, do not invite your friends or your brothers or your relatives or rich neighbors, lest they also invite you in return, and you be repaid. But when you give a feast, invite the poor, the maimed, the lame, the blind, and you will be blessed, because they cannot repay you" (*Lk* 14:12-14).

28. The Lord's appeal to show mercy to the poor culminates in the great parable of the last judgment (cf. *Mt* 25:31-46), which can serve as a vivid illustration of the Beatitude of the merciful. In that parable, the Lord offers us the key to our fulfillment in life; indeed, "if we seek the holiness pleasing to God's eyes, this text offers us one clear criterion on which we will be judged."[76] The clear and forceful words of the Gospel must be put into practice "without any 'ifs or buts' that could lessen their force. Our Lord made it very clear that holiness cannot be understood or lived apart from these demands."[77]

29. In the early Christian community, acts of charity were performed on the basis not of preliminary studies or advance planning, but directly following Jesus' example as presented in the Gospel. The Letter of James deals at length with the problem of relations between rich and poor, and asks the faithful two questions in order to examine the authenticity of their faith: "What good is it, my brothers and sisters, if you say you have faith but do not have works? Can faith save you? If a brother or sister is naked and lacks daily food, and one of you says to them, 'Go in peace; keep warm and eat your fill,' and yet you do not supply their bodily needs, what is the good of that? So faith by itself, if it has no works, is dead" (2:14-17).

30. James goes on to say: "Your gold and silver have rusted, and their rust will be evidence against you, and it will eat your flesh like fire. You have laid up treasure for the last days. Listen! The wages of the laborers who mowed your fields, which you kept back by fraud, cry out, and the cries of the harvesters have reached the ears of the Lord of hosts. You have lived on the earth in luxury and in pleasure; you have fattened your hearts in a day of slaughter"

(5:3-5). These are powerful words, even if we would rather not hear them! A similar appeal can be found in the First Letter of John: "How does God's love abide in anyone who has the world's goods and sees a brother or sister in need and yet refuses help?" (3:17).

31. The message of God's word is "so clear and direct, so simple and eloquent, that no ecclesial interpretation has the right to relativize it. The Church's reflection on these texts ought not to obscure or weaken their force, but urge us to accept their exhortations with courage and zeal. Why complicate something so simple? Conceptual tools exist to heighten contact with the realities they seek to explain, not to distance us from them."[78]

32. Indeed, we find a clear ecclesial example of sharing goods and caring for the poor in the daily life of the first Christian community. We can recall in particular the way in which the question of the daily distribution of subsidies to widows was resolved (cf. *Acts* 6:1-6). This was not an easy problem, partly because some of these widows, who came from other countries, were sometimes neglected because they were foreigners. In fact, the episode recounted in the Acts of the Apostles highlights a certain discontent on the part of the Hellenists, the Jews who were culturally Greek. The Apostles do not respond with abstract words, but by placing charity towards all at the center, reorganizing assistance to widows by asking the community to seek wise and respected people to whom they could entrust food distribution, while they take care of preaching the Word.

33. When Paul went to Jerusalem to consult the Apostles lest somehow he "should be running or had run in vain" (*Gal* 2:2), he was asked not to forget the poor (cf. *Gal* 2:10). Therefore, he organized various collections in order to help the poor communities. Among the reasons for which Paul makes this gesture, the following stands out: "God loves a cheerful giver" (*2 Cor* 9:7). The word of God reminds those of us not normally prone to benevolent and disinterested gestures, that generosity to the poor actually benefits those who exercise it: God has a special love for them. In fact, the Bible is full of promises addressed to those who give generously to others: "Whoever is kind to the poor lends to the Lord, and will be repaid in full" (*Prov* 19:17). "Give, and it will be given to you… for the measure you give will be the measure you get back" (*Lk* 6:38). "Then your light shall break forth like the dawn, and your healing shall spring up quickly" (*Is* 58:8). Of this, the early Christians had no doubt.

34. The life of the first ecclesial communities, described in the pages of the Bible and handed down to us as God's revealed word, has been given to us as an example to imitate, but also as a witness to the faith that works through charity and an enduring inspiration for generations yet to come. Throughout the centuries, those pages have moved the hearts of Christians to love and to perform works of charity, which, like fruitful seeds, never cease to produce a rich harvest.

CHAPTER THREE

A CHURCH FOR THE POOR

35. Three days after his election, my predecessor expressed to the representatives of the media his desire that care and attention for the poor be more clearly present in the Church: "How I would like a Church which is poor and for the poor!"[79]

36. This desire reflects the understanding that the Church "recognizes in those who are poor and who suffer, the likeness of its poor and suffering founder."[80] Indeed, since the Church is called to identify with those who are least, at her core "[T]here can be no room for doubt or for explanations which weaken so clear a message... We have to state, without mincing words, that there is an inseparable bond between our faith and the poor."[81] In this regard, we have numerous witnesses from disciples of Christ spanning almost two millennia.[82]

THE TRUE RICHES OF THE CHURCH

37. Saint Paul recounts that among the faithful of the nascent Christian community not many were "wise according to the flesh, not many were powerful, not many were of noble birth" (*1 Cor* 1:26). However, despite their poverty, the early Christians were clearly aware of the necessity to care for those who were most in need. Already at the dawn of Christianity, the Apostles laid their hands on seven men chosen from the community. To a certain extent, they integrated them into their own ministry, instituting them for the service—*diakonía* in Greek—of the poorest (cf. *Acts* 6:1-5). It is significant that the first disciple to bear witness to his faith in Christ to the point of shedding his blood was Stephen, who belonged to this group. In him, the witness of caring for the poor and of martyrdom are united.

38. A little less than two centuries later, another deacon, Saint Lawrence, will demonstrate his fidelity to Jesus Christ in a similar way by uniting martyrdom and service to the poor.[83] From Saint Ambrose's account, we learn that Lawrence, a deacon in Rome during the pontificate of Pope Sixtus II, was forced by the Roman authorities to turn over the treasures of the Church. "The following day he brought the poor with him. Questioned about where the promised treasures might be, he pointed to the poor saying,

'These are the treasures of the Church.'"[84] While narrating this event, Saint Ambrose asks: "What treasures does Jesus have that are more precious than those in which he loves to show himself?"[85] And, remembering that ministers of the Church must never neglect the care of the poor, much less accumulate goods for their own benefit, he says: "This task must be carried out with sincere faith and wise foresight. Certainly, if anyone derives personal advantage from it, he commits a crime; but if he distributes the proceeds to the poor or redeems a prisoner, he performs a work of mercy."[86]

THE FATHERS OF THE CHURCH AND THE POOR

39. From the first centuries, the Fathers of the Church recognized in the poor a privileged way to reach God, a special way to meet him. Charity shown to those in need was not only seen as a moral virtue, but a concrete expression of faith in the incarnate Word. The community of the faithful, sustained by the strength of the Holy Spirit, was rooted in being close to the poor, whom they considered not just an "appendage," but an essential part of Christ's living body. For example, while he was on his way to face martyrdom, Saint Ignatius of Antioch exhorted the community of Smyrna not to neglect the duty to carry out acts of charity for those most in need, admonishing them not to behave like those who oppose God. "But consider those who are of a different opinion with respect to the grace of Christ, which has come to us, how opposed they are to the will of God. They have no regard for love; no care for the widow, or the orphan, or the oppressed; of the bond, or of the free; of the hungry, or of the thirsty."[87] The Bishop of Smyrna, Polycarp, expressly stated that ministers of the Church should take care of the poor: "And let the presbyters be compassionate and merciful to all, bringing back those that wander, visiting all the sick, and not neglecting the widow, the orphan, or the poor, but always 'providing for that which is becoming in the sight of God and man.'"[88] From these two witnesses, we see that the Church appears as a mother of the poor, a place of welcome and justice.

40. For his part, Saint Justin, who addressed his First Apology to Emperor Adrian, the Senate and people of Rome, explained that Christians bring all that they can to those in need because they see them as brothers and sisters in Christ. Writing about the assembly gathered in prayer on the first day of the week, he underscored that at the heart of the Christian liturgy, it is not possible to separate the worship of God from concern for the poor. Consequently, at a certain point in the celebration: "they who are well-to-do, and willing, give what each thinks fit; and what is collected is deposited with the president, who succors the orphans and widows, and those who, through sickness or any other cause, are in want, and those who are in bonds, and the strangers sojourning among us, and in a word takes care of all who are in need."[89] This demonstrates that the nascent Church did not separate belief from social action: faith without witness through concrete actions was considered dead, as Saint James taught us (cf. 2:17).

Saint John Chrysostom

41. Among the Eastern Fathers, perhaps the most ardent preacher on social justice was Saint John Chrysostom, Archbishop of Constantinople from the late 300s to the early 400s. In his homilies, he exhorted the faithful to recognize Christ in the needy: "Do you wish to honor the body of Christ? Do not allow it to be despised in its members, that is, in the poor, who have no clothes to cover themselves. Do not honor Christ's body here in church with silk fabrics, while outside you neglect it when it suffers from cold and nakedness... [The body of Christ on the altar] does not need cloaks, but pure souls; while the one outside needs much care. Let us therefore learn to think of and honor Christ as he wishes. For the most pleasing honor we can give to the one we want to venerate is that of doing what he himself desires, not what we devise... So you too, give him the honor he has commanded, and let the poor benefit from your riches. God does not need golden vessels, but golden souls."[90] Affirming with crystal clarity that, if the faithful do not encounter Christ in the poor who stand at the door, they will not be able to worship him even at the altar, he continues: "What advantage does Christ gain if the sacrificial table is laden with golden vessels, while he himself dies of hunger in the person of the poor? Feed the hungry first, and only afterward adorn the altar with what remains."[91] He understood the Eucharist, therefore, as a sacramental expression of the charity and justice that both preceded and accompanied it. That same charity and justice should perpetuate the Eucharist through love and attention to the poor.

42. Consequently, charity is not optional but a requirement of true worship. Chrysostom vehemently denounced excessive wealth connected with indifference for the poor. The attention due to them, rather than a mere social requirement, is a condition for salvation, which gives unjust wealth a condemnatory weight. "It is very cold and the poor man lies in rags, dying, freezing, shivering, with an appearance and clothing that should move you. You, however, red in the face and drunk, pass by. And how do you expect God to deliver you from misfortune?... You often adorn an unfeeling corpse, which no longer understands honor, with many varied and gilded garments. Yet you despise the one who feels pain, who is torn apart, tortured, tormented by hunger and cold."[92] This profound sense of social justice leads him to affirm that "not giving to the poor is stealing from them, defrauding them of their lives, because what we have belongs to them."[93]

Saint Augustine

43. Augustine's spiritual guide was Saint Ambrose, who insisted on the ethical requirement to share material goods: "What you give to the poor is not your property, but theirs. Why have you appropriated what was given for common use?"[94] For the Bishop of Milan, almsgiving is justice restored, not a gesture of paternalism. In his preaching, mercy takes on a prophetic character: he denounces structures that accumulate things and reaffirms communion as the Church's vocation.

44. Formed in this tradition, the holy Bishop of Hippo taught for his part about the preferential love for the poor. A vigilant pastor and theologian of rare insight, he realizes that true ecclesial communion is expressed also in the communion of goods. In his Commentaries on the Psalms, he reminds us that true Christians do not neglect love for those most in need: "Observing your brothers and sisters, you know if they are in need, but if Christ dwells in you, also be charitable to strangers."[95] This sharing of goods therefore stems from theological charity and has as its ultimate goal the love of Christ. For Augustine, the poor are not just people to be helped, but the sacramental presence of the Lord.

45. The Doctor of Grace saw caring for the poor as concrete proof of the sincerity of faith. Anyone who says they love God and has no compassion for the needy is lying (cf. *1 Jn* 4:20). Commenting on Jesus' encounter with the rich young man and the "treasure in heaven" reserved for those who give their possessions to the poor (cf. *Mt* 19:21), Augustine puts the following words in the Lord's mouth: "I received the earth, I will give heaven; I received temporal goods, I will give back eternal goods; I received bread, I will give life... I have been given hospitality, but I will give a home; I was visited when I was sick, but I will give health; I was visited in prison, but I will give freedom. The bread you have given to my poor has been consumed, but the bread I will give will not only refresh you, but will never end."[96] The Almighty will not be outdone in generosity to those who serve the people most in need: the greater the love for the poor, the greater the reward from God.

46. This Christocentric and deeply ecclesial perspective leads us to affirm that offerings, when born of love, not only alleviate the needs of one's brother or sister, but also purify the heart of the giver, if he or she is willing to change. Indeed, in the words of Pseudo-Augustine: "almsgiving can be beneficial to you in erasing past sins, if you have amended your ways."[97] It is, so to speak, the ordinary path to conversion for those who wish to follow Christ with an undivided heart.

47. In a Church that recognizes in the poor the face of Christ and in material goods the instrument of charity, Augustine's thought remains a sure light. Today, fidelity to Augustine's teachings requires not only the study of his works, but also a readiness to live radically his call to conversion, which necessarily includes the service of charity.

48. Many other Fathers of the Church, both Eastern and Western, have spoken about the primacy of attention to the poor in the life and mission of every Christian. From this perspective, in summary, it can be said that patristic theology was practical, aiming at a Church that was poor and for the poor, recalling that the Gospel is proclaimed correctly only when it impels us to touch the flesh of the least among us, and warning that doctrinal rigor without mercy is empty talk.

CARE OF THE SICK

49. Christian compassion has manifested itself in a particular way in the care of the sick and suffering. Based on the signs present in Jesus' public ministry—the healing of the blind, lepers and paralytics—the Church understands that caring for the sick, in whom she readily recognizes the crucified Lord, is an important part of her mission. During a plague in the city of Carthage, where he was Bishop, Saint Cyprian reminded Christians of the importance of caring for the sick: "This pestilence and plague, which seems so horrible and deadly, searches out the righteousness of each one, and examines the minds of the human race, to see whether the healthy serve the sick; whether relatives love each other with sincerity; whether masters have pity on their sick servants; whether doctors do not abandon the sick who beg for help."[98] The Christian tradition of visiting the sick, washing their wounds, and comforting the afflicted is not simply a philanthropic endeavor, but an ecclesial action through which the members of the Church "touch the suffering flesh of Christ."[99]

50. In the sixteenth century, Saint John of God founded the Hospitaller Order that bears his name, creating model hospitals that welcomed everyone, regardless of social or economic status. His famous expression, "Do good, my brothers!" became a motto for active charity towards the sick. At the same time, Saint Camillus de Lellis founded the Order of Ministers of the Sick—the Camillians—taking on the mission of serving the sick with total dedication. His rule commands: "Each person should ask the Lord for a motherly affection for their neighbor so that we may serve them with all charity, both in soul and body, because we desire, with the grace of God, to serve all the sick with the affection that a loving mother has for her only sick child."[100] In hospitals, on battlefields, in prisons, and on the streets, the Camillians have embodied the mercy of Christ the Physician.

51. Caring for the sick with maternal affection, as a mother cares for her child, many consecrated women have played an even greater role in providing healthcare to the poor. The Daughters of Charity of Saint Vincent de Paul, the Hospital Sisters, the Little Sisters of Divine Providence, and many other women's congregations have become a maternal and discreet presence in hospitals, nursing homes and retirement homes. They have brought comfort, a listening ear, a presence, and above all, tenderness. They have built, often with their own hands, healthcare facilities in areas lacking medical assistance. They taught hygiene, assisted in childbirth and administered medicine with natural wisdom and deep faith. Their homes became oases of dignity where no one was excluded. The touch of compassion was the first medicine. Saint Louise de Marillac wrote to her sisters, the Daughters of Charity, reminding them that "they have been singularly blessed by God for the service of the sick poor of the hospitals."[101]

52. Today, this legacy continues in Catholic hospitals, healthcare facilities in remote areas, clinics operating in jungles, shelters for drug addicts and in field hospitals in war zones. The Christian presence among the sick reveals that salvation is not an abstract idea, but concrete action. In the act of healing a wound, the Church proclaims that the Kingdom of God begins among the most vulnerable. In doing so, she remains faithful to the One who said, "I was sick and you visited me" (*Mt* 25:36). When the Church kneels beside a leper, a malnourished child or an anonymous dying person, she fulfills her deepest vocation: to love the Lord where he is most disfigured.

CARE OF THE POOR IN MONASTIC LIFE

53. Monastic life, which originated in the silence of the desert, was from the outset a witness to solidarity. Monks and nuns left everything—wealth, prestige, family—not only because they despised worldly goods—*contemptus mundi*—but also to encounter the poor Christ in this radical detachment. Saint Basil the Great, in his Rule, saw no contradiction between the monks' life of prayer and contemplation and their work on behalf of the poor. For him, hospitality and care for the needy were an integral part of monastic spirituality, and monks, even after having left everything to embrace poverty, had to help the poorest with their work, because "in order to have enough to help the needy... it is clear that we must work diligently... This way of life is profitable not only for subduing the body, but also for charity towards our neighbor, so that through us God may provide enough for our weaker brothers and sisters."[102]

54. In Caesarea, where he was Bishop, he built a place known as *Basiliad*, which included lodgings, hospitals and schools for the poor and sick. The monk, therefore, was not only an ascetic, but also a servant. Basil thus demonstrated that to be close to God, one must be close to the poor. Concrete love was the criterion of holiness. Praying and caring, contemplating and healing, writing and welcoming: everything was an expression of the same love for Christ.

55. In the West, Saint Benedict of Norcia formulated a Rule that would become the backbone of European monastic spirituality. Welcoming the poor and pilgrims occupies a prominent place in the document: "The poor and pilgrims are to be received with all care and hospitality, for it is in them that Christ is received."[103] These were not just words: for centuries Benedictine monasteries were places of refuge for widows, abandoned children, pilgrims and beggars. For Benedict, community life was a school of charity. Manual labor not only had a practical function, but also formed the heart for service. Sharing among the monks, caring for the sick and listening to the most vulnerable prepared them to welcome Christ who comes in the person of the poor and the stranger. Today, Benedictine monastic hospitality remains a sign of a Church that opens its doors, welcomes without asking and heals without demanding anything in return.

56. Over time, Benedictine monasteries became places for overcoming the culture of exclusion. Monks and nuns cultivated the land, produced food, prepared medicines and offered them, with simplicity, to those most in need. Their silent work was the leaven of a new civilization, where the poor were not a problem to be solved, but brothers and sisters to be welcomed. The rule of sharing, working together and helping the vulnerable established an economy of solidarity, in contrast to the logic of accumulation. The monks' witness showed that voluntary poverty, far from being misery, is a path of freedom and communion. They did not limit themselves to helping the poor: they became their neighbors, brothers and sisters in the same Lord. In the cells and cloisters, they created a mysticism of God's presence in the little ones.

57. In addition to providing material assistance, monasteries played a fundamental role in the cultural and spiritual formation of the humblest. In times of plague, war and famine, they were places where the needy found bread and medicine, but also dignity and a voice. It was there that orphans were educated, apprentices received training and ordinary people were taught agricultural techniques and how to read. Knowledge was shared as a gift and a responsibility. The abbot was both teacher and father, and the monastic school was a place of freedom through truth. Indeed, as John Cassian writes, the monk must be characterized by "humility of heart... which leads not to knowledge that puffs up, but to knowledge that enlightens through the fullness of charity."[104] By forming consciences and transmitting wisdom, monks contributed to a Christian pedagogy of inclusion. Culture, marked by faith, was shared with simplicity. Knowledge, illuminated by charity, became service. Monastic life thus revealed itself as a style of holiness and a concrete way to transform society.

58. The monastic tradition teaches us that prayer and charity, silence and service, cells and hospitals form a single spiritual fabric. The monastery is a place of listening and action, of worship and sharing. Saint Bernard of Clairvaux, the great Cistercian reformer, "firmly recalled the need for a sober and measured life, in the refectory as in monastic clothing and buildings, recommending the support and care of the poor."[105] For him, compassion was not an option, but the true path of following Christ. Monastic life, therefore, if faithful to its original vocation, shows that the Church is fully the bride of the Lord only when she is also the sister of the poor. The cloister is not only a refuge from the world, but a school where one learns to serve it better. Where monks and nuns have opened their doors to the poor, the Church has revealed with humility and firmness that contemplation does not exclude mercy, but demands it as its purest fruit.

Freeing prisoners

59. Since apostolic times, the Church has seen the liberation of the oppressed as a sign of the Kingdom of God. Jesus himself proclaimed at the beginning of his public ministry: "The Spirit of the Lord is upon me, because he has anointed me to bring good news to the poor. He has sent me to proclaim release to the captives" (*Lk* 4:18). The early Christians, even in precarious conditions, prayed for and assisted their brothers and sisters who were prisoners, as the Acts of the Apostles (cf. 12:5; 24:23) and various writings of the Fathers attest. This mission of liberation has continued throughout the centuries through concrete actions, especially when the tragedy of slavery and imprisonment has marked entire societies.

60. Between the late twelfth and the early thirteenth centuries, when many Christians were captured in the Mediterranean or enslaved in wars, two religious orders arose: the Order of the Most Holy Trinity and of the Captives (Trinitarians), founded by Saint John of Matha and Saint Felix of Valois, and the Order of the Blessed Virgin Mary of Mercy (Mercedarians), founded by Saint Peter Nolasco with the support of the Dominican Saint Raymond of Peñafort. These communities of consecrated persons were born with the specific charism of freeing Christians who had been enslaved, placing their own possessions at the disposal of the enslaved[106] and many times offering their own lives in exchange. The Trinitarians, with their motto *Gloria tibi Trinitas et captivis libertas* (Glory to you, O Trinity, and liberty to the captives), and the Mercedarians, who added a fourth vow[107] to the religious vows of poverty, chastity and obedience, testified that charity can be heroic. The liberation of prisoners is an expression of Trinitarian love: a God who frees not only from spiritual slavery but also from concrete oppression. The act of rescuing someone from slavery and captivity is seen as an extension of Christ's redemptive sacrifice, whose blood is the price of our redemption (cf. *1 Cor* 6:20).

61. The original spirituality of these orders was deeply rooted in contemplation of the cross. Christ is the Redeemer of prisoners *par excellence*, and the Church, his Body, prolongs this mystery in time.[108] Religious did not see redemption as a political or economic action, but as a quasi-liturgical act, the sacramental offering of themselves. Many gave their own bodies to replace prisoners, literally fulfilling the commandment: "No one has greater love than this, to lay down one's life for one's friends" (*Jn* 15:13). The tradition of these orders did not come to an end. On the contrary, it inspired new forms of action in the face of modern forms of slavery: human trafficking, forced labor, sexual exploitation and various forms of dependency.[109] Christian charity is liberating when it becomes incarnate. Likewise, the mission of the Church, when she is faithful to her Lord, is at all times to proclaim liberation. Even today, when "millions of people—children, women and men of all ages—are deprived of their freedom and forced to live in conditions akin to slavery,"[110] this legacy is carried on by these orders and other institutions and congregations working in urban peripheries, conflict zones and migration routes. When the Church bends down to break the new chains that bind the poor, she becomes a paschal sign.

62. We cannot conclude this reflection on people deprived of their freedom without mentioning those in various prisons and detention centers. In this regard, we recall the words that Pope Francis addressed to a group of prisoners: "For me, entering a prison is always an important moment, because prison is a place of great humanity... Humanity that is tried, sometimes worn down by difficulties, guilt, judgments, misunderstandings, suffering, but at the same time full of strength, desire for forgiveness, and a desire for redemption."[111] This desire, among other things, has also been taken up by the orders devoted to the ransom of prisoners as a preferential service to the Church. As Saint Paul proclaimed: "For freedom Christ has set us free" (*Gal* 5:1). This freedom is not only interior: it manifests itself in history as love that cares for and frees us from every bond of slavery.

Witnesses of Evangelical Poverty

63. In the thirteenth century, faced with the growth of cities, the concentration of wealth and the emergence of new forms of poverty, the Holy Spirit gave rise to a new type of consecration in the Church: the mendicant orders. Unlike the stable monastic model, mendicants adopted an itinerant life, without personal or communal property, entrusting themselves entirely to providence. They did not merely serve the poor: they made themselves poor with them. They saw the city as a new desert and the marginalized as new spiritual teachers. These orders, such as the Franciscans, Dominicans, Augustinians and Carmelites, represented an evangelical revolution, in which a simple and poor lifestyle became a prophetic sign for mission, reviving the experience of the first Christian community (cf. *Acts* 4:32). The witness of the mendicants challenged both clerical opulence and the coldness of urban society.

64. Saint Francis of Assisi became the icon of this spiritual springtime. By embracing poverty, he wanted to imitate Christ, who was poor, naked and crucified. In his Rule, he asks that "the brothers should not appropriate anything, neither house, nor place, nor anything else. And as pilgrims and strangers in this world, serving the Lord in poverty and humility, they should go about begging with confidence, and should not be ashamed, because the Lord made himself poor for us in this world."[112] His life was one of continuous self-emptying: from the palace to the leper, from eloquence to silence, from possession to total gift. Francis did not found a social service organization, but an evangelical fraternity. In the poor, he saw brothers and sisters, living images of the Lord. His mission was to be with them, and he did so through a solidarity that overcame distances and a compassionate love. Francis' poverty was relational: it led him to become neighbor, equal to, or indeed lesser than others. His holiness sprang from the conviction that Christ can only be truly received by giving oneself generously to one's brothers and sisters.

65. Saint Clare of Assisi, who was inspired by Francis, founded the Order of Poor Ladies, later called the Poor Clares. Her spiritual struggle consisted in faithfully maintaining the ideal of radical poverty. She refused the papal privileges that could have guaranteed material security for her monastery and, with firmness, obtained from Pope Gregory IX the so-called *Privilegium Paupertatis*, which guaranteed the right to live without any material goods.[113] This choice expressed her total trust in God and her awareness that voluntary poverty was a form of freedom and prophecy. Clare taught her sisters that Christ was their only inheritance and that nothing should obscure their communion with him. Her prayerful and hidden life was a cry against worldliness and a silent defense of the poor and forgotten.

66. Saint Dominic de Guzmán, a contemporary of Francis, founded the Order of Preachers, with a different charism but the same radicalism of life. He wanted to proclaim the Gospel with the authority that comes from a life of poverty, convinced that the Truth needs witnesses of integrity. The example of poverty in their lives accompanied the Word they preached. Free from the weight of earthly goods, the Dominican Friars were better able to dedicate themselves to their principal work of preaching. They went to the cities, especially the universities, in order to teach the truth about God.[114] In their dependence on others, they showed that faith is not imposed but offered. And by living among the poor, they learned the truth of the Gospel "from below," as disciples of the humiliated Christ.

67. The mendicant orders were therefore a living response to exclusion and indifference. They did not expressly propose social reforms, but an individual and communal conversion to the logic of the Kingdom. For them, poverty was not a consequence of a scarcity of goods, but a free choice: to make themselves small in order to welcome the small. As Thomas of Celano said of Francis: "He showed that he loved the poor intensely... He often stripped himself naked to clothe the poor, whom he sought to resemble."[115] Beggars became the symbol of a pilgrim, humble and fraternal Church, living among the poor not to proselytize but as an expression of their true identity. They teach us that the Church is a light when she strips herself of everything, and that holiness passes through a humble heart devoted to the least among us.

The Church and the education of the poor

68. Addressing educators, Pope Francis recalled that education has always been one of the highest expressions of Christian charity: "Yours is a mission full of obstacles as well as joys... A mission of love, because you cannot teach without loving."[116] In this sense, since ancient times, Christians have understood that knowledge liberates, gives dignity, and brings us closer to the truth. For the Church, teaching the poor was an act of justice and faith. Inspired by the example of the Master who taught people divine and human truths, she took on the mission of forming children and young people, especially the poorest, in truth and love. This mission took shape with the founding of congregations dedicated to education.

69. In the sixteenth century, Saint Joseph Calasanz, struck by the lack of education and training among the poor young people of Rome, established Europe's first free public school in some rooms adjacent to the church of Santa Dorotea in Trastevere. This was the seed from which the Poor Clerics Regular of the Mother of God of the Pious Schools, known as the Piarists, would later emerge and develop, though not without difficulty. Their goal was that of transmitting to young people "not only secular knowledge but also the wisdom of the Gospel, teaching them to recognize, in their personal lives and in history, the loving action of God the Creator and Redeemer."[117] In fact, we can consider this courageous priest as the "true founder of the modern Catholic school, aimed at the integral formation of people and open to all."[118] Inspired by the same sensitivity, Saint John Baptist de La Salle, realizing the injustice caused by the exclusion of the children of workers and ordinary people from the educational system of France at that time, founded the Brothers of the Christian Schools in the seventeenth century, with the ideal of offering them free education, solid formation, and a fraternal environment. De La Salle saw the classroom as a place for human development, but also for conversion. In his colleges, prayer, method, discipline and sharing were combined. Each child was considered a unique gift from God, and the act of teaching was a service to the Kingdom of God.

70. In the nineteenth century, also in France, Saint Marcellin Champagnat founded the Institute of the Marist Brothers of the Schools. "He was sensitive to the spiritual and educational needs of his time, especially to religious ignorance and the situation of neglect experienced in a particular way by the young."[119] He dedicated himself wholeheartedly to the mission of educating and evangelizing children and young people, especially those most in need, during a period when access to education continued to be the privilege of a few. In the same spirit, Saint John Bosco began the great work of the Salesians in Italy based on the three principles of the "preventive method"—reason, religion, and loving kindness.[120] Blessed Antonio Rosmini founded the Institute of Charity, in which "intellectual charity" was placed alongside "material charity," with "spiritual-pastoral charity" at the top, as an indispensable dimension of any charitable action aimed at the good and integral development of the person.[121]

71. Many female congregations were protagonists of this pedagogical revolution. Founded in the eighteenth and nineteenth centuries, the Ursulines, the Sisters of the Company of Mary Our Lady, the Maestre Pie and many others, stepped into the spaces where the state was absent. They created schools in small villages, suburbs and working-class neighborhoods. In particular, the education of girls became a priority. The religious sisters taught literacy, evangelized, took care of practical matters of daily life, elevated their spirits through the cultivation of the arts, and, above all, formed consciences. Their pedagogy was simple: closeness, patience and gentleness. They taught by the example of their lives before teaching with words. In times of widespread illiteracy and systemic exclusion, these consecrated women were beacons of hope. Their mission was to form hearts, teach people to think and promote dignity. By combining a life of piety and dedication to others, they fought abandonment with the tenderness of those who educate in the name of Christ.

72. For the Christian faith, the education of the poor is not a favor but a duty. Children have a right to knowledge as a fundamental requirement for the recognition of human dignity. Teaching them affirms their value, giving them the tools to transform their reality. Christian tradition considers knowledge a gift from God and a community responsibility. Christian education does not only form professionals, but also people open to goodness, beauty and truth. Catholic schools, therefore, when they are faithful to their name, are places of inclusion, integral formation and human development. By combining faith and culture, they sow the seeds of the future, honor the image of God and build a better society.

Accompanying migrants

73. The experience of migration accompanies the history of the People of God. Abraham sets out without knowing where he is going; Moses leads the pilgrim people through the desert; Mary and Joseph flee with the child Jesus to Egypt. Christ himself, who "came to what was his own, and his own people did not accept him" (*Jn* 1:11), lived among us as a stranger. For this reason, the Church has always recognized in migrants a living presence of the Lord who, on the day of judgment, will say to those on his right: "I was a stranger and you welcomed me" (*Mt* 25:35).

74. In the nineteenth century, when millions of Europeans emigrated in search of better living conditions, two great saints distinguished themselves in the pastoral care of migrants: Saint John Baptist Scalabrini and Saint Frances Xavier Cabrini. Scalabrini, Bishop of Piacenza, founded the Missionaries of Saint Charles to accompany migrants to their destinations, offering them spiritual, legal and material assistance. He saw migrants as recipients of a new evangelization, warning of the risks of exploitation and loss of faith in a foreign land. Responding generously to the charism that the Lord had given him, "Scalabrini looked forward to a world and a Church without barriers, where no one was a foreigner."[122] Saint Frances Cabrini, born in Italy and a naturalized American, was the first citizen of the United States of America to be canonized. To fulfill her mission of assisting migrants, she crossed the Atlantic several times. "Armed with remarkable boldness, she started schools, hospitals and orphanages from nothing for the masses of the poor who ventured into the new world in search of work. Not knowing the language and lacking the wherewithal to find a respectable place in American society, they were often victims of the unscrupulous. Her motherly heart, which allowed her no rest, reached out to them everywhere: in hovels, prisons and mines."[123] In the Holy Year of 1950, Pope Pius XII proclaimed her Patroness of All Migrants.[124]

75. The Church's tradition of working for and with migrants continues, and today this service is expressed in initiatives such as refugee reception centers, border missions and the efforts of Caritas Internationalis and other institutions. Contemporary teaching clearly reaffirms this commitment. Pope Francis has recalled that the Church's mission to migrants and refugees is even broader, insisting that "our response to the challenges posed by contemporary migration can be summed up in four verbs: welcome, protect, promote and integrate. Yet these verbs do not apply only to migrants and refugees. They describe the Church's mission to all those living in the existential peripheries, who need to be welcomed, protected, promoted and integrated."[125] He also said: "Every human being is a child of God! He or she bears the image of Christ! We ourselves need to see, and then to enable others to see, that migrants and refugees do not only represent a problem to be solved, but are brothers and sisters to be welcomed, respected and loved. They are an occasion that Providence gives us to help build a more just society, a more perfect democracy, a more united country, a more fraternal world and a more open and evangelical Christian community."[126] The Church, like a mother, accompanies those who are walking. Where the world sees threats, she sees children; where walls are built, she builds bridges. She knows that her proclamation of the Gospel is credible only when it is translated into gestures of closeness and welcome. And she knows that in every rejected migrant, it is Christ himself who knocks at the door of the community.

At the side of the least among us

76. Christian holiness often flourishes in the most forgotten and wounded places of humanity. The poorest of the poor—those who lack not only material goods but also a voice and the recognition of their dignity—have a special place in God's heart. They are the beloved of the Gospel, the heirs to the Kingdom (cf. Lk 6:20). It is in them that Christ continues to suffer and rise again. It is in them that the Church rediscovers her call to show her most authentic self.

77. Saint Teresa of Calcutta, canonized in 2016, has become a universal icon of charity lived to the fullest extent in favor of the most destitute, those discarded by society. Foundress of the Missionaries of Charity, she dedicated her life to the dying abandoned on the streets of India. She gathered the rejected, washed their wounds and accompanied them to the moment of death with the tenderness of prayer. Her love for the poorest of the poor meant that she did not only take care of their material needs, but also proclaimed the good news of the Gospel to them: "We are wanting to proclaim the good news to the poor that God loves them, that we love them, that they are somebody to us, that they too have been created by the same loving hand of God, to love and to be loved. Our poor people are great people, are very lovable people, they do not need our pity and sympathy, they need our understanding love. They need our respect; they need that we treat them with dignity."[127] All this came from a deep spirituality that saw service to the poorest as the fruit of prayer and love, the source of true peace, as Pope John Paul II reminded the pilgrims who came to Rome for her beatification: "Where did Mother Teresa find the strength to place herself completely at the service of others? She found it in prayer and in the silent contemplation of Jesus Christ, his Holy Face, his Sacred Heart. She herself said as much: 'The fruit of silence is prayer; the fruit of prayer is faith; the fruit of faith is love; the fruit of love is service.' It was prayer that filled her heart with Christ's own peace and enabled her to radiate that peace to others."[128] Teresa did not consider herself a philanthropist or an activist, but a bride of Christ crucified, serving with total love her suffering brothers and sisters.

78. In Brazil, Saint Dulce of the Poor—known as "the good angel of Bahia"—embodied the same evangelical spirit with Brazilian characteristics. Referring to her and two other religious women canonized during the same celebration, Pope Francis recalled their love for the most marginalized members of society and said that the new saints "show us that the consecrated life is a journey of love at the existential peripheries of the world."[129] Sister Dulce responded to precariousness with creativity, obstacles with tenderness and need with unshakeable faith. She began by taking in the sick in a chicken coop and from there founded one of the largest social services in the country. She assisted thousands of people a day, without ever losing her gentleness, making herself poor with the poor for the love of the Poorest One. She lived with little, prayed fervently and served with joy. Her faith did not distance her from the world, but drew her even more deeply into the pain of the least among us.

79. We could also mention individuals such as Saint Benedict Menni and the Sisters Hospitallers of the Sacred Heart of Jesus, who worked alongside people with disabilities; Saint Charles de Foucauld among the communities of the Sahara; Saint Katharine Drexel for the most underprivileged groups in North America; Sister Emmanuelle, with the garbage collectors in the Ezbet El Nakhl neighborhood of Cairo; and many others. Each in their own way discovered that the poorest are not only objects of our compassion, but teachers of the Gospel. It is not a question of "bringing" God to them, but of encountering him among them. All of these examples teach us that serving the poor is not a gesture to be made "from above," but an encounter between equals, where Christ is revealed and adored. Saint John Paul II reminded us that "there is a special presence of Christ in the poor, and this requires the Church to make a preferential option for them."[130] Therefore, when the Church bends down to care for the poor, she assumes her highest posture.

Popular Movements

80. We must also recognize that, throughout centuries of Christian history, helping the poor and advocating for their rights has not only involved individuals, families, institutions, or religious communities. There have been, and still are, various popular movements made up of lay people and led by popular leaders, who have often been viewed with suspicion and even persecuted. I am referring to "all those persons who journey, not as individuals, but as a closely-bound community of all and for all, one that refuses to leave the poor and vulnerable behind... 'Popular' leaders, then, are those able to involve everyone... They do not shun or fear those young people who have experienced hurt or borne the weight of the cross."[131]

81. These popular leaders know that solidarity "also means fighting against the structural causes of poverty and inequality; of the lack of work, land and housing; and of the denial of social and labor rights. It means confronting the destructive effects of the empire of money... Solidarity, understood in its deepest sense, is a way of making history, and this is what the popular movements are doing."[132] For this reason, when different institutions think about the needs of the poor, it is necessary to "include popular movements and invigorate local, national and international governing structures with that torrent of moral energy that springs from including the excluded in the building of a common destiny."[133] Popular movements, in fact, invite us to overcome "the idea of social policies being a policy for the poor, but never with the poor and never of the poor, much less part of a project which can bring people back together."[134] If politicians and professionals do not listen to them, "democracy atrophies, turns into a slogan, a formality; it loses its representative character and becomes disembodied, since it leaves out the people in their daily struggle for dignity, in the building of their future."[135] The same must be said of the institutions of the Church.

CHAPTER 4

A HISTORY THAT CONTINUES

The century of the Church's Social Doctrine

82. The acceleration of technological and social change in the past two centuries, with all its contradictions and conflicts, not only had an impact on the lives of the poor but also became the object of debate and reflection on their part. The various movements of workers, women and young people, and the fight against racial discrimination, gave rise to a new appreciation of the dignity of those on the margins of society. The Church's social doctrine also emerged from this matrix. Its analysis of Christian revelation in the context of modern social, labor, economic and cultural issues would not have been possible without the contribution of the laity, men and women alike, who grappled with the great issues of their time. At their side were those men and women religious who embodied a Church forging ahead in new directions. The epochal change we are now undergoing makes even more necessary a constant interaction between the faithful and the Church's Magisterium, between ordinary citizens and experts, between individuals and institutions. Here too, it needs to be acknowledged once more that reality is best viewed from the sidelines, and that the poor are possessed of unique insights indispensable to the Church and to humanity as a whole.

83. The Church's Magisterium in the past 150 years is a veritable treasury of significant teachings concerning the poor. The Bishops of Rome have given voice to new insights refined through a process of ecclesial discernment. By way of example, in his Encyclical Letter *Rerum Novarum*, Leo XIII addressed the labor question, pointing to the intolerable living conditions of many industrial workers and arguing for the establishment of a just social order. Other popes also spoke on this theme. Saint John XXIII, in his Encyclical *Mater et Magistra* (1961), called for justice on a global scale: rich countries could no longer remain indifferent to countries suffering from hunger and extreme poverty; instead, they were called upon to assist them generously with all their goods.

84. The Second Vatican Council represented a milestone in the Church's understanding of the poor in God's saving plan. Although this theme remained marginal in the preparatory documents, Saint John XXIII, in his Radio Message of 11 September 1962, a month before the opening of the Council, called attention to the issue. In his memorable words, "the Church presents herself as she is and as she wishes to be: the Church of all and in particular the Church of the poor."[136] The intense efforts of bishops, theologians and experts concerned with the renewal of the Church—with the support of Saint John XXIII himself—gave the Council a new direction. The centrality of Christ in these considerations both on a doctrinal and social level would prove fundamental. Many

Council Fathers supported this approach, as eloquently expressed by Cardinal Lercaro in his intervention of 6 December 1962: "The mystery of Christ in the Church has always been and today is, in a particular way, the mystery of Christ in the poor."[137] He went on to say that, "this is not simply one theme among others, but in some sense the only theme of the Council as a whole."[138] The Archbishop of Bologna, in preparing the text for this intervention, noted the following: "This is the hour of the poor, of the millions of the poor throughout the world. This is the hour of the mystery of the Church as mother of the poor. This is the hour of the mystery of Christ, present especially in the poor."[139] There was a growing sense of the need for a new image of Church, one simpler and more sober, embracing the entire people of God and its presence in history. A Church more closely resembling her Lord than worldly powers and working to foster a concrete commitment on the part of all humanity to solving the immense problem of poverty in the world.

85. At the opening of the second session of the Council, Saint Paul VI took up this concern voiced by his predecessor, namely that the Church looks with particular attention "to the poor, the needy, the afflicted, the hungry, the suffering, the imprisoned, that is, she looks to all humanity that suffers and weeps: she is part of them by evangelical right."[140] In his General Audience of 11 November 1964, he pointed out that "the poor are representatives of Christ," and compared the image of the Lord in the poor to that seen in the Pope. He affirmed this truth with these words: "The representation of Christ in the poor is universal; every poor person reflects Christ; that of the Pope is personal... The poor man and Peter can be one in the same person, clothed in a double representation; that of poverty and that of authority."[141] In this way, the intrinsic link between the Church and the poor was expressed symbolically and with unprecedented clarity.

86. The Pastoral Constitution *Gaudium et Spes*, building on the teachings of the Church Fathers, forcefully reaffirms the universal destination of earthly goods and the social function of property that derives from it. The Constitution states that "God destined the earth and all it contains for all people and nations so that all created things would be shared fairly by all humankind under the guidance of justice tempered by charity... In their use of things people should regard the external goods they lawfully possess as not just their own but common to others as well, in the sense that they can benefit others as well as themselves. Therefore, everyone has the right to possess a sufficient amount of the earth's goods for themselves and their family... Persons in extreme necessity are entitled to take what they need from the riches of others... By its nature, private property has a social dimension that is based on the law of the common destination of earthly goods. Whenever the social aspect is forgotten, ownership can often become the object of greed and a source of serious disorder."[142] This conviction was reiterated by Saint Paul VI in his Encyclical *Populorum Progressio*. There we read that no one can feel authorized to "appropriate surplus goods solely for his [or her] own private use when others lack the bare necessities of life."[143] In his address to the United Nations, Pope Paul VI spoke as the advocate of poor peoples[144] and urged the international community to build a world of solidarity.

87. With Saint John Paul II, the Church's preferential relationship with the poor was consolidated, particularly from a doctrinal standpoint. His teaching saw in the option for the poor a "special form of primacy in the exercise of Christian charity, to which the whole tradition of the Church bears witness."[145] In his Encyclical *Sollicitudo Rei Socialis*, he went on to say: "Today, furthermore, given the worldwide dimension which the social question has assumed, this love of preference for the poor, and the decisions which it inspires in us, cannot but embrace the immense multitudes of the hungry, the needy, the homeless, those without medical care and, above all, those without hope of a better future. It is impossible not to take account of the existence of these realities. To ignore them would mean becoming like the 'rich man' who pretended not to know the beggar Lazarus lying at his gate (cf. *Lk* 16:19-31)."[146] Saint John Paul II's teaching on work is likewise important for our consideration of the active role that the poor ought to play in the renewal of the Church and society, thus leaving behind a certain "paternalism" that limited itself to satisfying only the immediate needs of the poor. In his Encyclical *Laborem Exercens*, he forthrightly stated that "human work is a key, probably the essential key, to the whole social question."[147]

88. Amid the multiple crises that marked the beginning of the third millennium, the teaching of Benedict XVI took a more distinctly political turn. Hence, in the Encyclical *Caritas in Veritate*, he affirms that "the more we strive to secure a common good corresponding to the real needs of our neighbors, the more effectively we love them."[148] He observed, moreover, that "hunger is not so much dependent on lack of material things as on shortage of social resources, the most important of which are institutional. What is missing, in other words, is a network of economic institutions capable of guaranteeing regular access to sufficient food and water for nutritional needs, and also capable of addressing the primary needs and necessities ensuing from genuine food crises, whether due to natural causes or political irresponsibility, nationally and internationally."[149]

89. Pope Francis recognized that in recent decades, alongside the teachings of the Bishops of Rome, national and regional Bishops' Conferences have increasingly spoken out. He could personally attest, for example, to the particular commitment of the Latin

American episcopate to rethinking the Church's relationship with the poor. In the immediate post-conciliar period, in almost all Latin American countries, there was a strong sense of the Church's need to identify with the poor and to participate actively in securing their freedom. The Church was moved by the masses of the poor suffering from unemployment, underemployment, unjust wages and sub-standard living conditions. The martyrdom of Saint Oscar Romero, the Archbishop of San Salvador, was a powerful witness and an inspiration for the Church. He had made his own the plight of the vast majority of his flock and made them the center of his pastoral vision. The Conferences of the Latin American Bishops held in Medellín, Puebla, Santo Domingo and Aparecida were also significant events for the life of the Church as a whole. For my part, having served as a missionary in Peru for many years, I am greatly indebted to this process of ecclesial discernment, which Pope Francis wisely linked to that of other particular Churches, especially those in the global South. I would now like to take up two specific themes of this episcopal teaching.

STRUCTURES OF SIN THAT CREATE POVERTY AND EXTREME INEQUALITY

90. At Medellín, the bishops declared themselves in favor of a preferential option for the poor: "Christ our Savior not only loved the poor, but, 'being rich, he became poor.' He lived a life of poverty, focused his mission on preaching their liberation, and founded his Church as a sign of this poverty in our midst... The poverty endured by so many of our brothers and sisters cries out for justice, solidarity, witness, commitment and efforts directed to ending it, so that the saving mission entrusted by Christ may be fully accomplished."[150] The bishops stated forcefully that the Church, to be fully faithful to her vocation, must not only share the condition of the poor, but also stand at their side and work actively for their integral development. Faced with a situation of worsening poverty in Latin America, the Puebla Conference confirmed the Medellín decision in favor of a frank and prophetic option for the poor and described structures of injustice as a "social sin."

91. Charity has the power to change reality; it is a genuine force for change in history. It is the source that must inspire and guide every effort to "resolve the structural causes of poverty,"[151] and to do so with urgency. It is my hope that we will see more and more "politicians capable of sincere and effective dialogue aimed at healing the deepest roots—and not simply the appearances—of the evils in our world."[152] For "it is a matter of hearing the cry of entire peoples, the poorest peoples of the earth."[153]

92. We must continue, then, to denounce the "dictatorship of an economy that kills," and to recognize that "while the earnings of a minority are growing exponentially, so too is the gap separating the majority from the prosperity enjoyed by those happy few. This imbalance is the result of ideologies that defend the absolute autonomy of the marketplace and financial speculation. Consequently, they reject the right of states, charged with vigilance for the common good, to exercise any form of control. A new tyranny is being born, invisible and often virtual, which unilaterally and relentlessly imposes its own laws and rules."[154] There is no shortage of theories attempting to justify the present state of affairs or to explain that economic thinking requires us to wait for invisible market forces to resolve everything. Nevertheless, the dignity of every human person must be respected today, not tomorrow, and the extreme poverty of all those to whom this dignity is denied should constantly weigh upon our consciences.

93. In his Encyclical *Dilexit Nos*, Pope Francis reminded us that social sin consolidates a "structure of sin" within society, and is frequently "part of a dominant mindset that considers normal or reasonable what is merely selfishness and indifference. This then gives rise to social alienation."[155] It then becomes normal to ignore the poor and live as if they do not exist. It then likewise seems reasonable to organize the economy in such a way that sacrifices are demanded of the masses in order to serve the needs of the powerful. Meanwhile, the poor are promised only a few "drops" that trickle down, until the next global crisis brings things back to where they were. A genuine form of alienation is present when we limit ourselves to theoretical excuses instead of seeking to resolve the concrete problems of those who suffer. Saint John Paul II had already observed that, "a society is alienated if its forms of social organization, production and consumption make it more difficult to offer the gift of self and to establish solidarity between people."[156]

94. We need to be increasingly committed to resolving the structural causes of poverty. This is a pressing need that "cannot be delayed, not only for the pragmatic reason of its urgency for the good order of society, but because society needs to be cured of a sickness which is weakening and frustrating it, and which can only lead to new crises. Welfare projects, which meet certain urgent needs, should be considered merely provisional responses."[157] I can only state once more that inequality "is the root of social ills."[158] Indeed, "it frequently becomes clear that, in practice, human rights are not equal for all."[159]

95. As it is, "the current model, with its emphasis on success and self-reliance, does not appear to favor an investment in efforts to help the slow, the weak or the less talented to find opportunities in life."[160] The same questions keep coming back to us. Does this mean that the less gifted are not human beings? Or that the weak do not have the same dignity as ourselves? Are those born with fewer opportunities of lesser value as human beings? Should they limit themselves merely to surviving? The worth of our societies, and our own future, depends on the answers we give to these questions. Either we regain our moral and spiritual dignity or we fall into a cesspool. Unless we stop and take this matter seriously, we will continue, openly or surreptitiously, "to legitimize the present model of distribution, where a minority believes that it has the right to consume in a way which can never be universalized, since the planet could not even contain the waste products of such consumption."[161]

96. One structural issue that cannot realistically be resolved from above and needs to be addressed as quickly as possible has to do with the locations, neighborhoods, homes and cities where the poor live and spend their time. All of us appreciate the beauty of "those cities which overcome paralyzing mistrust, integrate those who are different and make this very integration a new factor of development! How attractive are those cities which, even in their architectural design, are full of spaces which connect, relate and favor the recognition of others!"[162] Yet, at the same time, "we cannot fail to consider the effects on people's lives of environmental deterioration, current models of development and the throwaway culture."[163] For "the deterioration of the environment and of society affects the most vulnerable people on the planet."[164]

97. All the members of the People of God have a duty to make their voices heard, albeit in different ways, in order to point out and denounce such structural issues, even at the cost of appearing foolish or naïve. Unjust structures need to be recognized and eradicated by the force of good, by changing mindsets but also, with the help of science and technology, by developing effective policies for societal change. It must never be forgotten that the Gospel message has to do not only with an individual's personal relationship with the Lord, but also with something greater: "the Kingdom of God (cf. *Lk* 4:43); it is about loving God who reigns in our world. To the extent that he reigns within us, the life of society will be a setting for universal fraternity, justice, peace and dignity. Both Christian preaching and life, then, are meant to have an impact on society. We are seeking God's Kingdom."[165]

98. Finally, in a document that was not initially well received by everyone, we find a reflection that remains timely today: "The defenders of orthodoxy are sometimes accused of passivity, indulgence, or culpable complicity regarding the intolerable situations of injustice and the political regimes which prolong them. Spiritual conversion, the intensity of the love of God and neighbor, zeal for justice and peace, the Gospel meaning of the poor and of poverty, are required of everyone, and especially of pastors and those in positions of responsibility. The concern for the purity of the faith demands giving the answer of effective witness in the service of one's neighbor, the poor and the oppressed in particular, in an integral theological fashion."[166]

THE POOR AS SUBJECTS

99. The life of the universal Church was enriched by the discernment of the Aparecida Conference, in which the Latin American bishops made clear that the Church's preferential option for the poor "is implicit in the Christological faith in the God who became poor for us, so as to enrich us with his poverty."[167] The Aparecida Document situates the Church's mission in the present context of a globalized world marked by new and dramatic imbalances.[168] In their Final Message, the bishops wrote: "The stark differences between rich and poor invite us to work with greater commitment to being disciples capable of sharing the table of life, the table of all the sons and daughters of the Father, a table that is open and inclusive, from which no one is excluded. We therefore reaffirm our preferential and evangelical option for the poor."[169]

100. At the same time, the Document, taking up a theme treated in earlier Conferences of the Latin American episcopate, insists on the need to consider marginalized communities as *subjects* capable of creating their own culture, rather than as *objects* of charity on the part of others. This means that such communities have the right to embrace the Gospel and to celebrate and communicate their faith in accord with the values present within their own cultures. Their experience of poverty gives them the ability to recognize aspects of reality that others cannot see; for this reason, society needs to listen to them. The same holds true for the Church, which should regard positively their "popular" practice of the faith. A fine passage from the Aparecida Document can help us reflect on this point and our proper response: "Only the closeness that makes us friends enables us to appreciate deeply the values of the poor today, their legitimate desires, and their own manner of living the faith... Day by day, the poor become agents of evangelization and of comprehensive human promotion: they educate their children in the faith, engage in ongoing solidarity among relatives and neighbors, constantly seek God, and give life to the Church's pilgrimage. In the light of the Gospel, we recognize their immense dignity and their sacred worth in the eyes of Christ, who was poor like them and excluded among them. Based on this experience of faith, we will share with them the defense of their rights."[170]

101. All this entails one aspect of the option for the poor that we must constantly keep in mind, namely that it demands of us an attitude of attentiveness to others. "This loving attentiveness is the beginning of a true concern for their person which inspires me effectively to seek their good. This entails appreciating the poor in their goodness, in their experience of life, in their culture, and in their ways of living the faith. True love is always contemplative, and permits us to serve the other not out of necessity or vanity, but rather because he or she is beautiful above and beyond mere appearances... Only on the basis of this real and sincere closeness can we properly accompany the poor on their path of liberation."[171] For this reason, I express my heartfelt gratitude to all those who have chosen to live among the poor, not merely to pay them an occasional visit but to live with them as they do. Such a decision should be deemed one of the highest forms of evangelical life.

102. In light of this, it is evident that all of us must "let ourselves be evangelized"[172] by the poor and acknowledge "the mysterious wisdom which God wishes to share with us through them."[173] Growing up in precarious circumstances, learning to survive in the most adverse conditions, trusting in God with the assurance that no one else takes them seriously, and helping one another in the darkest moments, the poor have learned many things that they keep hidden in their hearts. Those of us who have not had similar experiences of living this way certainly have much to gain from the source of wisdom that is the experience of the poor. Only by relating our complaints to their sufferings and privations can we experience a reproof that can challenge us to simplify our lives.

CHAPTER FIVE

A CONSTANT CHALLENGE

103. I have chosen to recall the age-old history of the Church's care for the poor and with the poor in order to make clear that it has always been a central part of her life. Indeed, caring for the poor is part of the Church's great Tradition, a beacon as it were of evangelical light to illumine the hearts and guide the decisions of Christians in every age. That is why we must feel bound to invite everyone to share in the light and life born of recognizing Christ in the faces of the suffering and those in need. Love for the poor is an essential element of the history of God's dealings with us; it rises up from the heart of the Church as a constant appeal to the hearts of the faithful, both individually and in our communities. As the Body of Christ, the Church experiences the lives of the poor as her very "flesh," for theirs is a privileged place within the pilgrim people of God. Consequently, love for the poor—whatever the form their poverty may take—is the evangelical hallmark of a Church faithful to the heart of God. Indeed, one of the priorities of every movement of renewal within the Church has always been a preferential concern for the poor. In this sense, her work with the poor differs in its inspiration and method from the work carried out by any other humanitarian organization.

104. No Christian can regard the poor simply as a societal problem; they are part of our "family." They are "one of us." Nor can our relationship to the poor be reduced to merely another ecclesial activity or function. In the words of the Aparecida Document, "we are asked to devote time to the poor, to give them loving attention, to listen to them with interest, to stand by them in difficult moments, choosing to spend hours, weeks or years of our lives with them, and striving to transform their situations, starting from them. We cannot forget that this is what Jesus himself proposed in his actions and by his words."[174]

The Good Samaritan, once again

105. The dominant culture at the beginning of this millennium would have us abandon the poor to their fate and consider them unworthy of attention, much less our respect. Pope Francis, in his Encyclical *Fratelli Tutti*, challenged us to reflect on the parable of the Good Samaritan (cf. *Lk* 10:25-37), which presents the different reactions of those confronted by the sight of a wounded man lying on the road. Only the Good Samaritan stops and cares for him. Pope Francis went on to ask each of us: "Which of these persons do you identify with? This question, blunt as it is, is direct and incisive. Which of these characters do you resemble? We need to acknowledge that we are constantly tempted to ignore others, especially the weak. Let us admit that, for all the progress we have made, we are still 'illiterate' when it comes to accompanying, caring for and supporting the most frail and vulnerable members of our developed societies. We have become accustomed to looking the other way, passing by, and ignoring situations until they affect us directly."[175]

106. It is important for us to realize that the story of the Good Samaritan remains timely even today. "If I encounter a person sleeping outdoors on a cold night, I can view him or her as an annoyance, an idler, an obstacle in my path, a troubling sight, a problem for politicians to sort out, or even a piece of refuse cluttering a public space. Or I can respond with faith and charity, and see in this person a human being with a dignity identical to my own, a creature infinitely loved by the Father, an image of God, a brother or sister redeemed by Jesus Christ. That is what it is to be a Christian! Can holiness somehow be understood apart from this lively recognition of the dignity of each human being?"[176] What did the Good Samaritan do?

107. These questions become all the more urgent in light of a serious flaw present in the life of our societies, but also in our Christian communities. The many forms of indifference we see all around us are in fact "signs of an approach to life that is spreading in various and subtle ways. What is more, caught up as we are with our own needs, the sight of a person who is suffering disturbs us. It makes us uneasy, since we have no time to waste on other people's problems. These are symptoms of an unhealthy society. A society that seeks prosperity but turns its back on suffering. May we not sink to such depths! Let us look to the example of the Good Samaritan."[177] The final words of the Gospel parable—"Go and do likewise" (*Lk* 10:37)—represent a mandate that every Christian must daily take to heart.

An inescapable challenge for the Church today

108. At a particularly critical time in the history of the Church in Rome, when the imperial institutions were collapsing under the pressure of the barbarian invasions, Pope Saint Gregory the Great felt it necessary to remind the faithful: "Every minute we can find a Lazarus if we seek him, and every day, even without seeking, we find one at our door. Now beggars besiege us, imploring alms; later they will be our advocates… Therefore do not waste the opportunity of doing works of mercy; do not store unused the good things you possess."[178] Gregory courageously denounced contemporary forms of prejudice against the poor, including the belief that they were responsible for their plight: "Whenever you see the poor doing something reprehensible, do not despise or discredit them, for the fire of poverty is perhaps purifying their sinful actions, however slight they be."[179] Not infrequently, our prosperity can make us blind to the needs of others, and even make us think that our happiness and fulfillment depend on ourselves alone, apart from others. In such cases, the poor can act as silent teachers for us, making us conscious of our presumption and instilling within us a rightful spirit of humility.

109. While it is true that the rich care for the poor, the opposite is no less true. This is a remarkable fact confirmed by the entire Christian tradition. Lives can actually be turned around by the realization that the poor have much to teach us about the Gospel and its demands. By their silent witness, they make us confront the precariousness of our existence. The elderly, for example, by their physical frailty, remind us of our own fragility, even as we attempt to conceal it behind our apparent prosperity and outward appearance. The poor, too, remind us how baseless is the attitude of aggressive arrogance with which we frequently confront life's difficulties. They remind us how uncertain and empty our seemingly safe and secure lives may be. Here again, Saint Gregory the Great has much to tell us: "Let no one consider himself secure, saying, 'I do not steal from others, but simply enjoy what is rightfully mine.' The rich man was not punished because he took what belonged to others, but because, while possessing such great riches, he had become impoverished within. This was indeed the reason for his condemnation to hell: in his prosperity, he preserved no sense of justice; the wealth he had received made him proud and caused him to lose all sense of compassion."[180]

110. For us Christians, the problem of the poor leads to the very heart of our faith. Saint John Paul II taught that the preferential option for the poor, namely the Church's love for the poor, "is essential for her and a part of her constant tradition, and impels her to give attention to a world in which poverty is threatening to assume massive proportions in spite of technological and economic progress."[181] For Christians, the poor are not a sociological category, but the very "flesh" of Christ. It is not enough to profess the doctrine of God's Incarnation in general terms. To enter truly into this great mystery, we need to understand clearly that the Lord took on a flesh that hungers and thirsts, and experiences infirmity and imprisonment. "A poor Church for the poor begins by reaching out to the flesh of Christ. If we reach out to the flesh of Christ, we begin to understand something, to understand what this poverty, the Lord's poverty, actually is; and this is far from easy." [182]

111. By her very nature the Church is in solidarity with the poor, the excluded, the marginalized and all those considered the outcast of society. The poor are at the heart of the Church because "our faith in Christ, who became poor, and was always close to the poor and the outcast, is the basis of our concern for the integral development of society's most neglected members."[183] In our hearts, we encounter "the need to heed this plea, born of the liberating action of grace within each of us, and so it is not a matter of a mission reserved only to a few."[184]

112. At times, Christian movements or groups have arisen which show little or no interest in the common good of society and, in particular, the protection and advancement of its most vulnerable and disadvantaged members. Yet we must never forget that religion, especially the Christian religion, cannot be limited to the private sphere, as if believers had no business making their voice heard with regard to problems affecting civil society and issues of concern to its members.[185]

113. Indeed, "any Church community, if it thinks it can comfortably go its own way without creative concern and effective cooperation in helping the poor to live with dignity and reaching out to everyone, will also risk breaking down, however much it may talk about social issues or criticize governments. It will easily drift into a spiritual worldliness camouflaged by religious practices, unproductive meetings and empty talk."[186]

114. Nor is it a question merely of providing for welfare assistance and working to ensure social justice. Christians should also be aware of another form of inconsistency in the way they treat the poor. In reality, "the worst discrimination which the poor suffer is the lack of spiritual care... Our preferential option for the poor must mainly translate into a privileged and preferential religious care."[187] Yet, this spiritual attentiveness to the poor is called into question, even among Christians, by certain prejudices arising from the fact that we find it easier to turn a blind eye to the poor. There are those who say: "Our task is to pray and teach sound doctrine." Separating this religious aspect from integral development, they even say that it is the government's job to care for them, or that it would be better not to lift them out of their poverty but simply to teach them to work. At times, pseudo-scientific data are invoked to support the claim that a free market economy will automatically solve the problem of poverty. Or even that we should opt for pastoral work with the so-called elite, since, rather than wasting time on the poor, it would be better to care for the rich, the influential and professionals, so that with their help real solutions can be found and the Church can feel protected. It is easy to perceive the worldliness behind these positions, which would lead us to view reality through superficial lenses, lacking any light from above, and to cultivate relationships that bring us security and a position of privilege.

Almsgiving today

115. I would like to close by saying something about almsgiving, which nowadays is not looked upon favorably even among believers. Not only is it rarely practiced, but it is even at times disparaged. Let me state once again that the most important way to help the disadvantaged is to assist them in finding a good job, so that they can lead a more dignified life by developing their abilities and contributing their fair share. In this sense, "lack of work means far more than simply not having a steady source of income. Work is also this, but it is much, much more. By working we become a fuller person, our humanity flourishes, young people become adults only by working. The Church's social doctrine has always seen human work as a participation in God's work of creation that continues every day, also thanks to the hands, mind and heart of the workers."[188] On the other hand, where this is not possible, we cannot risk abandoning others to the fate of lacking the necessities for a dignified life. Consequently, almsgiving remains, for the time being, a necessary means of contact, encounter and empathy with those less fortunate.

116. Those inspired by true charity know full well that almsgiving does not absolve the competent authorities of their responsibilities, eliminate the duty of government institutions to care for the poor, or detract from rightful efforts to ensure justice. Almsgiving at least offers us a chance to halt before the poor, to look into their eyes, to touch them and to share something of ourselves with them. In any event, almsgiving, however modest, brings a touch of *pietas* into a society otherwise marked by the frenetic pursuit of personal gain. In the words of the Book of Proverbs: "Those who are generous are blessed, for they share their bread with the poor" (22:9).

117. Both the Old and New Testaments contain veritable hymns in praise of almsgiving: "Be patient with someone in humble circumstances, and do not keep him waiting for your alms... Store up almsgiving in your treasury, and it will rescue you from every disaster" (*Sir* 29:8,12). Jesus himself adds: "Sell your possessions, and give alms. Make purses for yourselves that do not wear out, an unfailing treasure in heaven, where no thief comes near and no moth destroys" (*Lk* 12:33).

118. Saint John Chrysostom is known for saying: "Almsgiving is the wing of prayer. If you do not provide your prayer with wings, it will hardly fly."[189] In the same vein, Saint Gregory of Nazianzus concluded one of his celebrated orations with these words: "If you think that I have something to say, servants of Christ, his brethren and co-heirs, let us visit Christ whenever we may; let us care for him, feed him, clothe him, welcome him, honor him, not only at a meal, as some have done, or by anointing him, as Mary did, or only by lending him a tomb, like Joseph of Arimathea, or by arranging for his burial, like Nicodemus, who loved Christ half-heartedly, or by giving him gold, frankincense and myrrh, like the Magi before all these others. The Lord of all asks for mercy, not sacrifice... Let us then show him mercy in the persons of the poor and those who today are lying on the ground, so that when we come to leave this world they may receive us into everlasting dwelling places."[190]

119. Our love and our deepest convictions need to be continually cultivated, and we do so through our concrete actions. Remaining in the realm of ideas and theories, while failing to give them expression through frequent and practical acts of charity, will eventually cause even our most cherished hopes and aspirations to weaken and fade away. For this very reason, we Christians must not abandon almsgiving. It can be done in different ways, and surely more effectively, but it must continue to be done. It is always better at least to do something rather than nothing. Whatever form it may take, almsgiving will touch and soften our hardened hearts. It will not solve the problem of world poverty, yet it must still be carried out, with intelligence, diligence and social responsibility. For our part, we need to give alms as a way of reaching out and touching the suffering flesh of the poor.

120. Christian love breaks down every barrier, brings close those who were distant, unites strangers, and reconciles enemies. It spans chasms that are humanly impossible to bridge, and it penetrates to the most hidden crevices of society. By its very nature, Christian love is prophetic: it works miracles and knows no limits. It makes what was apparently impossible happen. Love is above all a way of looking at life and a way of living it. A Church that sets no limits to love, that knows no enemies to fight but only men and women to love, is the Church that the world needs today.

121. Through your work, your efforts to change unjust social structures or your simple, heartfelt gesture of closeness and support, the poor will come to realize that Jesus' words are addressed personally to each of them: "I have loved you" (*Rev* 3:9).

122. *Given in Rome, at Saint Peter's, on October 4, the Memorial of Saint Francis of Assisi, in the year 2025, the first of my Pontificate.*

Notes

(1) Pope Leo XIV, *Urbi et Orbi*, May 8, 2025, https://www.vatican.va/content/leo-xiv/en/messages/urbi/documents/20250508-prima-benedizione-urbietorbi.html.

(2) Pope Leo XIV, Homily in the Crypt of Saint Peter's Basilica, May 11, 2025, https://www.vatican.va/content/leo-xiv/en/homilies/2025/documents/20250511-messa-grotte-vaticane.html.

(3) Bahman Dehgan, *America in Quotations* (Jefferson, North Carolina: McFarland, 2015), 28.

(4) Vatican News, "Biography of Pope Leo XIV, Born Robert Francis Prevost," https://www.vaticannews.va/en/pope/news/2025-05/biography-of-robert-francis-prevost-pope-leo-xiv.html.

(5) Belinda Luscombe, "The Making of an American Pope," *Time*, July 2, 2025, https://time.com/7298083/pope-leo-xiv-robert-prevost-american/.

(6) Ibid.

(7) Ibid.

(8) Ibid.

(9) Ibid.

(10) Ibid.

(11) Ibid.

(12) Ibid.

(13) Ibid.

(14) Jordana Comiter, "Meet Pope Leo XIV's Family: All about His Parents and Brothers (and Their Chicago Roots!)," *People*, May 9, 2025, https://people.com/all-about-pope-leo-xiv-family-11731662.

(15) Camillo Barone and Brian Roewe, "Top Augustinians and Friends of Leo XIV Reflect on Relationship with Former Boss," *National Catholic Reporter*, May 12, 2025, https://www.ncronline.org/news/top-augustinians-and-friends-leo-xiv-reflect-relationship-former-boss.

(16) Brendan Towell, "An Augustinian for These Times: A Personal Reflection on Meeting Cardinal Robert Prevost, OSA," The Augustinians, https://augustinian.org/an-augustinian-for-these-times-cardinal-robert-prevost-osa/.

(17) Pope Leo XIV, Homily, June 1, 2025, https://www.vatican.va/content/leo-xiv/en/homilies/2025/documents/20250601-omelia-giubileo-famiglie.html.

(18) Ruth Graham and Julie Bosman, "Pope's Childhood in a Changing Chicago Tells a Story of Catholic America," *The New York Times*, May 10,

2025, https://www.nytimes.com/2025/05/10/us/pope-leo-childhood-chicago-catholics.html.

(19) "Pope Leo Dialogues with Children: 'Build Bridges from an Early Age," *Vatican News*, https://www.vaticannews.va/en/pope/news/2025-07/pope-leo-dialogues-with-children-build-bridges-from-early-age.html.

(20) Ibid.

(21) Nicole Winfield, "Pope Speaks about Childhood and Early Mornings as an Altar Boy in Unscripted Visit with Campers, AP News, https://apnews.com/article/pope-leo-childhood-chicago-mass-ukrainians-76c5f0699057ad99a5309ba8170f75d7.

(22) Pope Leo XIV, Address to the Seminarians of the Dioceses of Triveneto, June 25, 2025, https://www.vatican.va/content/leo-xiv/en/speeches/2025/june/documents/20250625-seminaristi-triveneto.html.

(23) Pope Leo XIV, Address to Participants in the Course for Formators in Seminaries and to Participants in the General Chapter of the Xaverian Brothers, July 25, 2025, https://www.vatican.va/content/leo-xiv/en/speeches/2025/july/documents/20250725-sacerdoti.html.

(24) St. Teresa of Ávila, *Life*, viii.

(25) Jonathon Woodyard, "10 Thoughts from St. Augustine on Friendship," *Theology Along the Way*, July 10, 2018, https://theologyalongtheway.org/2018/07/10/10-thoughts-from-st-augustine-on-friendship/.

(26) St. Augustine, *Sermons (341-400) on Various Subjects* (Hyde Park, New York: New City Press, 1996), 388.

(27) Order of Saint Augustine, "Interview with Cardinal Robert Prevost OSA: 'Above All, a Bishop Must Proclaim Jesus Christ,'" https://www.augustinianorder.org/post/interview-with-cardinal-robert-prevost-osa-above-all-a-bishop-must-proclaim-jesus-christ.

(28) Pope Leo XIV, *Urbi et Orbi*, May 8, 2025, https://www.vatican.va/content/leo-xiv/en/messages/urbi/documents/20250508-prima-benedizione-urbietorbi.html.

(29) James K. A. Smith, "What to Expect from an Augustinian Pope," *America*, May 12, 2025, https://www.americamagazine.org/faith/2025/05/12/smith-augustinian-pope-leo-250662/.

(30) "Pope Leo XIV's Motto and Coat of Arms," Vatican News, https://www.vaticannews.va/en/pope/news/2025-05/pope-leo-xiv-s-motto-and-coat-of-arms.html.

(31) Ibid.

(32) Gregory Grimes, "The Augustinian Roots of Pope Leo XIV," *Church Life Journal*, May 13, 2025, https://churchlifejournal.nd.edu/articles/the-augustinian-roots-of-pope-leo-xiv/.

Notes

(33) USCCB, "Full Text of 2012 CNS Interview with Future Pope Leo XIV on New Evangelization," *Catholic News Service*, May 14, 2025, https://www.usccb.org/news/2025/full-text-2012-cns-interview-future-pope-leo-xiv-new-evangelization.

(34) Pope Leo XIV, "Video Message to the Augustinian Province of St. Thomas of Villanova," August 29, 2025, https://www.vatican.va/content/leo-xiv/en/messages/pont-messages/2025/documents/20250829-videomessaggio-santommaso-davillanova.html.

(35) Andrea Tornielli, "Archbishop Prevost: 'The Bishop Is a Pastor, Not a Manager," *Vatican News*, https://www.vaticannews.va/en/vatican-city/news/2023-05/archbishop-prevost-the-bishop-is-a-pastor-not-a-manager.html.

(36) Pope John Paul II, *Redemtoris Missio*, December 7, 1990, https://www.vatican.va/content/john-paul-ii/en/encyclicals/documents/hf_jp-ii_enc_07121990_redemptoris-missio.html, 2, 3.

(37) Order of Saint Augustine, "Interview with Cardinal Robert Prevost OSA: 'Above All, a Bishop Must Proclaim Jesus Christ,'" https://www.augustinianorder.org/post/interview-with-cardinal-robert-prevost-osa-above-all-a-bishop-must-proclaim-jesus-christ.

(38) Pope Leo XIV, *Urbi et Orbi*, May 8, 2025, https://www.vatican.va/content/leo-xiv/en/messages/urbi/documents/20250508-prima-benedizione-urbietorbi.html.

(39) Ibid.

(40) Pope Leo XIV, Homily, May 18, 2025, https://www.vatican.va/content/leo-xiv/en/homilies/2025/documents/20250518-inizio-pontificato.html.

(41) Pope Leo XIV, Address to Pontifical Mission Societies, May 22, 2025, https://www.vatican.va/content/leo-xiv/en/speeches/2025/may/documents/20250522-pom.html.

(42) Pope Leo XIV, Address to the College of Cardinals, May 10, 2025, https://www.vatican.va/content/leo-xiv/en/speeches/2025/may/documents/20250510-collegio-cardinalizio.html.

(43) Pope Leo XIV, Homily, May 18, 2025, https://www.vatican.va/content/leo-xiv/en/homilies/2025/documents/20250518-inizio-pontificato.html.

(44) Pope Leo XIV, *Regina Caeli*, May 11, 2025, https://www.vatican.va/content/leo-xiv/en/angelus/2025/documents/20250511-regina-caeli.html.

(45) Fr. Robert F. Prevost, OSA, "The Servant Leader in the Perspective of Augustinian Spirituality," Order of Saint Augustine, July 25, 2005, https://img1.wsimg.com/blobby/go/b07573f7-7ff1-4b22-9390-9a52a5a0dbbc/downloads/cb3db544-5655-493f-bd92-8cb9a0e0ac25/Prevost%20-%20Augustinian%20Servant%20Leadership%20-%20200.pdf?ver=1728850567405.

(46) Ibid.

(47) Ibid.

(48) Ibid.

(49) Pope Leo XIV, Address to the Italian Episcopal Conference, June 17, 2025, https://www.vatican.va/content/leo-xiv/en/speeches/2025/june/documents/20250617-cei.html.

(50) Kathleen N. Hattrup, "Peace: the Pope's 1st Wish, with Some 100 Mentions in 100 Days," *Aleteia*, August 9, 2025, https://aleteia.org/2025/08/09/peace-the-popes-1st-wish-with-some-100-mentions-in-100-days/.

(51) Pope Leo XIV, Homily, May 11, 2025, https://www.vatican.va/content/leo-xiv/en/homilies/2025/documents/20250511-messa-grotte-vaticane.html.

(52) Hugo of Saint Victor, *Explanation of the Rule of Saint Augustine* (Aeterna Press, 2008).

(53) Pope Leo XIV, Homily, May 18, 2025, https://www.vatican.va/content/leo-xiv/en/homilies/2025/documents/20250518-inizio-pontificato.html.

(54) Pope Leo XIV, Address to the Moderators of Lay Associations, Ecclesial Movements and New Communities, June 6, 2025, https://www.vatican.va/content/leo-xiv/en/speeches/2025/june/documents/20250606-moderatori.html.

(55) Pope Francis, *Spes Non Confundit*, May 9, 2024, https://www.vatican.va/content/francesco/en/bulls/documents/20240509_spes-non-confundit_bolla-giubileo2025.html.

(56) USCCB, "Full Text: Pope Leo XIV's Address to the Young People of Chicago and the Whole World," June 14, 2025, https://www.usccb.org/news/2025/full-text-pope-leo-xivs-address-young-people-chicago-and-whole-world.

(57) Pope Leo XIV, Message for the Fifth World Day of Grandparents and the Elderly, July 27, 2025, https://press.vatican.va/content/salastampa/en/bollettino/pubblico/2025/07/10/250710b.html.

(58) Pope Leo XIV, General Audience, August 27, 2025, https://www.vatican.va/content/leo-xiv/en/audiences/2025/documents/20250827-udienza-generale.html.

(59) Pope Benedict XVI, *Spe Salvi*, November 30, 2007, https://www.vatican.va/content/benedict-xvi/en/encyclicals/documents/hf_ben-xvi_enc_20071130_spe-salvi.html.

(60) Order of Saint Augustine, "Interview with Cardinal Robert Prevost OSA: 'Above All, a Bishop Must Proclaim Jesus Christ,'" https://www.augustinianorder.org/post/interview-with-cardinal-robert-prevost-osa-above-all-a-bishop-must-proclaim-jesus-christ.

(61) Francis, Encyclical Letter *Dilexit Nos* (24 October 2024), 170: AAS 116 (2024), 1422.

(62) Ibid., 171: AAS 116 (2024), 1422-1423.

(63) Francis, Apostolic Exhortation *Gaudete et Exsultate* (19 March 2018), 96: AAS 110 (2018), 1137.

(64) Francis, Audience with Representatives of the Communications Media (16 March 2013): AAS 105 (2013), 381.

(65) J. Bergoglio - A. Skorka, *Sobre el cielo y la tierra*, Buenos Aires 2013, 214.

(66) Paul VI, Homily at the Mass for the Last Public Session of the Second Vatican Ecumenical Council (7 December 1965): AAS 58 (1966), 55-56.

(67) Cf. Francis, Apostolic Exhortation *Evangelii Gaudium* (24 November 2013), 187: AAS 105 (2013), 1098.

(68) Ibid., 212: AAS 105 (2013), 1108.

(69) Francis, Encyclical Letter *Fratelli* Tutti (3 October 2020), 23: AAS 112 (2020), 977.

(70) Ibid., 21: AAS 112 (2020), 976.

(71) Council of the European Communities, *Decision (85/8/EEC) on Specific Community Action to Combat Poverty* (19 December 1984), Art. 1(2): *Official Journal of the European Communities*, No. L 2/24.

(72) Cf. John Paul II, *Catechesis* (27 October 1999): *L'Osservatore Romano*, 28 October 1999, 4.

(73) Francis, Apostolic Exhortation *Evangelii Gaudium* (24 November 2013), 197: AAS 105 (2013), 1102.

(74) Cf. Francis, Message for the 5th World Day of the Poor (13 June 2021), 3: AAS 113 (2021), 691: "Jesus not only sides with the poor; he also shares their lot. This is a powerful lesson for his disciples in every age."

(75) Francis, Apostolic Exhortation *Evangelii Gaudium* (24 November 2013), 186: AAS 105 (2013), 1098.

(76) Francis, Apostolic Exhortation *Gaudete et Exsultate* (19 March 2018), 95: AAS 110 (2018), 1137.

(77) Ibid., 97: AAS 110 (2018), 1137.

(78) Francis, Apostolic Exhortation *Evangelii Gaudium* (24 November 2013), 194: AAS 105 (2013), 1101.

(79) Francis, Audience with Representatives of the Communications Media (16 March 2013): AAS 105 (2013), 381.

(80) Second Vatican Ecumenical Council, Dogmatic Constitution *Lumen Gentium*, 8.

(81) Francis, Apostolic Exhortation *Evangelii Gaudium* (24 November 2013), 48: AAS 105 (2013), 1040.

(82) In this chapter, some of these witnesses are being put forward. This is not being done in an exhaustive manner but rather to demonstrate that care for the poor has always characterized the presence of the Church in the world. A more in-depth reflection on the attention given to those most in need can be found in the following book: V. Paglia, *Storia della povertà*, Milan 2014.

(83) Cf. Ambrose, *De officiis ministrorum* I, cap. 41, 205-206: CCSL 15, Turnhout 2000, 76-77; II, cap. 28, 140-143: CCSL 15, 148-149.

(84) Ibid., II, cap. 28, 140: CCSL 15, 148.

(85) Ibid.

(86) Ibid., II, cap. 28, 142: CCSL 15, 148.

(87) Ignatius of Antioch, *Epistula ad Smyrnaeo*s, 6, 2: SC 10bis, Paris 2007, 136-138.

(88) Polycarp, *Epistula ad Philippenses*, 6, 1: SC 10bis, 186.

(89) Justin, *Apologia prima*, 67, 6-7: SC 507, Paris 2006, 310.

(90) John Chrysostom, *Homiliae in Matthaeum*, 50, 3: PG 58, Paris 1862, 508.

(91) Ibid. 50, 4: PG 58, 509.

(92) John Chrysostom, *Homilia in Epistula ad Hebraeos*, 11, 3: PG 63, Paris 1862, 94.

(93) John Chrysostom, *Homilia II De Lazaro*, 6: PG 48, Paris 1862, 992.

(94) Ambrose, *De Nabuthae*, 12, 53: CSEL 32/2, Prague-Vienna-Leipzig 1897, 498.

(95) Augustine, *Enarrationes in Psalmos*, 125, 12: CSEL 95/3, Vienna 2001, 181.

(96) Augustine, *Sermo LXXXVI*, 5: CCSL 41Ab, Turnhout 2019, 411-412.

(97) Pseudo-Augustine, *Sermo CCCLXXXVIII*, 2: PL 39, Paris 1862, 1700.

(98) Cyprian, *De mortalitate*, 16: CCSL 3A, Turnhout 1976, 25.

(99) Francis, Message for the 30th World Day of the Sick (10 December 2021), 3: AAS 114 (2022), 51.

(100) Camillus de Lellis, *Rule of the Order of Ministers of the Sick*, 27: M. Vanti (ed.), Scritti di San Camillo de Lellis, Milan 1965, 67.

(101) Louise de Marillac, *Letter to Sisters Claudia Carré and Maria Gaudoin* (28 November 1657): E. Charpy (ed.), *Sainte Louise de Marillac. Écrits*, Paris 1983, 576.

(102) Basil the Great, *Regulae fusius tractatae*, 37, 1: PG 31, Paris 1857, 1009 C-D.

(103) *Regula Benedicti, 53*, 15: SC 182, Paris 1972, 614.

(104) John Cassian, *Collationes*, XIV, 10: CSEL 13, Vienna 2004, 410.

(105) Benedict XVI, *Catechesis* (21 October 2009): L'Osservatore Romano, 22 October 2009, 1.

(106) Cf. Innocent III, Bull *Operante divinae dispositionis – Primitive Rule of the Trinitarians* (17 December 1198), 2: J.L. Aurrecoechea – A. Moldón (eds.), Fuentes históricas de la Orden Trinitaria (s. XII-XV), Córdoba 2003, 6: "All things, from whatever lawful source they may come, the brothers are to divide them into three equal parts. Insofar as two parts will be sufficient, the works of mercy are to be performed from them, as well as providing for a moderate sustenance for themselves and their necessary household members. The third part is to be reserved for the ransom of captives who are incarcerated for the faith of Christ."

(107) Cf. *Constitutions of the Mercedarian Order*, n. 14: Orden de la Bienaventurada Virgen María de la Merced, Regla y Constituciones, Rome 2014, 53: "To fulfill this mission, driven by charity, we consecrate ourselves to God with a special vow, called Redemption, by virtue of which we promise to give our lives, if necessary, as Christ gave his for us, to save Christians who are in extreme danger of losing their faith in new forms of slavery."

(108) Cf. Saint John Baptist of the Conception, *La regla de la Orden de la Santísima Trinidad*, XX, 1: BAC Maior 60, Madrid, 1999, 90: "In this, the poor and prisoners are like Christ, on whom the sufferings of the world are laid... This holy Order of the Most Holy Trinity summons them and invites them to come and drink the water of the Savior, which means that, if Christ hanging on the cross was redemption and salvation for men, the Order has taken this redemption and wants to distribute it to the poor and save and free the prisoners."

(109) Cf. Saint John Baptist of the Conception, *El recogimiento interior*, XL, 4: BAC Maior 48, Madrid 1995, 689: "Free will makes man free and master among all creatures, but, God help me, how many are those who, by this way, become slaves and prisoners of the devil, imprisoned and chained by their passions and lusts."

(110) Francis, Message for the 48th World Day of Peace (8 December 2014), 3: AAS 107 (2015), 69.

(111) Francis, Meeting with Police Prison Officers, Detainees, and Volunteers (Verona, May 18 May 2024): AAS 116 (2024), 766.

(112) Honorius III, *Bull Solet annuere – Regula bullata* (29 November 1223), chap. VI: SC 285, Paris 1981, 192.

(113) Cf. Gregory IX, Bull *Sicut manifestum est* (17 September 1228), 7: SC 325, Paris 1985, 200: "Sicut igitur supplicastis, altissimae paupertatis propositum vestrum favore apostolico roboramus, auctoritate vobis praesentium indulgentes, ut recipere possessiones a nullo compelli possitis."

(114) Cf. S.C. Tugwell, (ed.), *Early Dominicans. Selected Writings*, Mahwah 1982, 16-19.

(115) Thomas of Celano, *Vita Seconda, pars prima*, cap. IV, 8: AnalFranc, 10, Florence 1941, 135.

(116) Francis, Address following the visit to the tomb of Don Lorenzo Milani, (Barbiana, 20 June 2017), 2: AAS 109 (2017), 745.

(117) John Paul II, Address to the Participants in the General Chapter of the Poor Clerics Regular of the Mother of God of the Pious Schools (Piarists) (5 July 1997), 2: L'Osservatore Romano, 6 July 1997, 5.

(118) Ibid.

(119) John Paul II, Homily for the Mass of Canonization (18 April 1999): AAS 91 (1999), 930.

(120) Cf. John Paul II, Letter *Iuvenum Patris* (31 January 1988), 9: AAS 80 (1988), 976.

(121) Cf. Francis, Address to the Participants in the General Chapter of the Institute of Charity (Rosminians) (1 October 2018): L'Osservatore Romano, 1-2 October 2018, 7.

(122) Francis, Homily for the Mass of Canonization (9 October 2022): AAS 114 (2022), 1338.

(123) John Paul II, Message to the Congregation of the Missionary Sisters of the Sacred Heart (31 May 2000), 3: *L'Osservatore Romano*, 16 July 2000, 5.

(124) Cf. Pius XII, Papal Brief Superior Iam Aetate (8 September 1950): AAS 43 (1951), 455-456.

(125) Francis, Message for the 105th World Day of Migrants and Refugees (27 May 2019): AAS 111 (2019), 911.

(126) Francis, Message for the 100th World Day of Migrants and Refugees (5 August 2013): AAS 105 (2013), 930.

(127) Teresa of Calcutta, Speech on the occasion of the awarding of the Nobel Peace Prize (Oslo, 10 December 1979): Aimer jusqu'à en avoir mal, Lyon 2017, 19-20.

(128) John Paul II, Address to the Pilgrims who had come to Rome for the Beatification of Mother Teresa (20 October 2003), 3: L'Osservatore Romano, 20-21 October 2003, 10.

(129) Francis, Homily for the Mass and Canonization (13 October 2019): AAS 111 (2019), 1712.

(130) John Paul II, Apostolic Letter *Novo Millennio Ineunte* (6 January 2001), 49: AAS 93 (2001), 302.

(131) Francis, Apostolic Exhortation *Christus Vivit* (25 March 2019), 231: AAS 111 (2019), 458.

(132) Francis, Address to Participants in the World Meeting of Popular Movements (28 October 2014): AAS 106 (2014), 851-852.

(133) Ibid.: AAS 106 (2014), 859.

(134) Francis, Address to Participants in the World Meeting of Popular Movements (November 5, 2016): *L'Osservatore Romano*, 7-8 November, 2016, 5.

(135) Ibid.

(136) John XXIII, Radio Message to all the Christian faithful one month before the opening of the Second Vatican Ecumenical Council (11 September 1962): AAS 54 (1962), 682.

(137) G. Lercaro, Intervention in the XXXV General Congregation of the Second Vatican Ecumenical Council (6 December 1962), 2: AS I/IV, 327-328.

(138) Ibid., 4: AS I/IV, 329.

(139) Institute for Religious Sciences (ed.), *Per la forza dello Spirito. Discorsi conciliari del Card. Giacomo Lercaro*, Bologna 1984, 115.

(140) Paul VI, Address for the Solemn Inauguration of the Second Session of the Second Vatican Ecumenical Council (29 September 1963): AAS 55 (1963) 857.

(141) Paul VI, Catechesis (11 November 1964): *Insegnamenti di Paolo VI*, II (1964), 984.

(142) Second Vatican Ecumenical Council, Pastoral Constitution *Gaudium et Spes*, 69, 71.

(143) Paul VI, Encyclical Letter *Populorum Progressio* (26 March 1967), 23: AAS 59 (1967), 269.

(144) Cf. ibid., 4: AAS 59 (1967), 259.

(145) John Paul II, Encyclical Letter Sollicitudo Rei Socialis (30 December 1987), 42: AAS 80 (1988), 572.

(146) Ibid., AAS 80 (1988), 573.

(147) John Paul II, Encyclical Letter *Laborem Exercens* (14 September 1981), 3: AAS 73 (1981), 584.

(148) Benedict XVI, Encyclical Letter *Caritas in Veritate* (29 June 2009), 7: AAS 101 (2009), 645.

(149) Ibid., 27: AAS 101 (2009), 661.

(150) Second General Conference of the Latin American Bishops, *Medellín Document* (24 October 1968), 14, n. 7: Celam, *Medellín. Conclusiones*, Lima 2005, 131-132.

(151) Francis, Apostolic Exhortation *Evangelii Gaudium* (24 November 2013), 202: AAS 105 (2013), 1105.

(152) Ibid., 205: AAS 105 (2013), 1106.

(153) Ibid., 190: AAS 105 (2013), 1099.

(154) Ibid., 56: AAS 105 (2013), 1043.

(155) Francis, Encyclical Letter *Dilexit Nos* (24 October 2024), 183: AAS 116 (2024), 1427.

(156) John Paul II, Encyclical Letter *Centesimus Annus* (1 May 1991), 41: AAS 83 (1991), 844-845.

(157) Francis, Apostolic Exhortation *Evangelii Gaudium* (24 November 2013), 202: AAS 105 (2013), 1105.

(158) Ibid.

(159) Francis, Encyclical Letter *Fratelli Tutti* (3 October 2020), 22: AAS 112 (2020), 976.

(160) Francis, Apostolic Exhortation *Evangelii Gaudium* (24 November 2013), 209: AAS 105 (2013), 1107.

(161) Francis, Encyclical Letter *Laudato Si'* (24 May 2015), 50: AAS 107 (2015), 866.

(162) Francis, Apostolic Exhortation *Evangelii Gaudium* (24 November 2013), 210: AAS 105 (2013), 1107.

(163) Francis, Encyclical Letter *Laudato Si'* (24 May 2015), 43: AAS 107 (2015), 863.

(164) Ibid., 48: AAS 107 (2015), 865.

(165) Francis, Apostolic Exhortation *Evangelii Gaudium* (24 November 2013), 180: AAS 105 (2013), 1095.

(166) Congregation for the Doctrine of the Faith, Instruction on Certain Aspects of the "Theology of Liberation" (6 August 1984) XI, 18: AAS 76 (1984), 907-908.

(167) Fifth General Conference of the Latin American and Caribbean Bishops, *Aparecida Document*, (29 June 2007), n. 392, Bogotá 2007, pp. 179-180. Cf. Benedict XVI, Address at the Inaugural Session of the Fifth General Conference of the Bishops of Latin America and the Caribbean (13 May 2007), 3: AAS 99 (2007), 450.

(168) Cf. Fifth General Conference of the Latin American and Caribbean Bishops, *Aparecida Document* (29 June 2007), nn. 43-87, pp. 31-47.

(169) Fifth General Conference of the Latin American and Caribbean Bishops, Final Message (29 May 2007), n. 4, Bogotá 2007, p. 275.

(170) Fifth General Conference of the Latin American and Caribbean Bishops, Aparecida Document (29 June 2007), n. 398, p. 182.

(171) Francis, Apostolic Exhortation *Evangelii Gaudium* (24 November 2013), 199: AAS 105 (2013), 1103-1104.

(172) Ibid., 198: AAS 105 (2013), 1103.

(173) Ibid.

(174) Fifth General Conference of the Bishops of Latin America and the Caribbean, *Aparecida Document* (29 June 2007), n. 397, p. 182.

(175) Francis, Encyclical Letter *Fratelli Tutti* (3 October 2020), 64: AAS 112 (2020), 992.

(176) Francis, Apostolic Exhortation *Gaudete et Exsultate* (19 March 2018), 98: AAS 110 (2018), 1137.

(177) Francis, Encyclical Letter *Fratelli Tutti* (3 October 2020), 65-66: AAS 112 (2020), 992.

(178) Gregory the Great, Homilia 40, 10: SC 522, Paris 2008, 552-554.

(179) Ibid., 6: SC 522, 546.

(180) Ibid., 3: SC 522, 536.

(181) John Paul II, Encyclical Letter *Centesimus Annus* (1 May 1991), 57: AAS 83 (1991), 862-863.

(182) Francis, Vigil of Pentecost with the Ecclesial Movements (18 May 2013): *L'Osservatore Romano* 20-21 May 2013, 5.

(183) Francis, Apostolic Exhortation *Evangelii Gaudium* (24 November 2013), 186: AAS 105 (2013), 1098.

(184) Ibid., 188: AAS 105 (2013), 1099.

(185) Cf. ibid., 182-183: AAS 105 (2013), 1096-1097.

(186) Ibid., 207: AAS 105 (2013), 1107.

(187) Ibid., 200: AAS 105 (2013), 1104.

(188) Francis, Address at the Meeting with Representatives of the World of Labor at the Ilva Factory in Genoa (27 May 2017): AAS 109 (2017), 613.

(189) Pseudo-Chrysostom, Homilia de Jejunio et Eleemosyna: PG 48, 1060.

(190) Gregory Nazianzus, *Oratio XIV*, 40: PG 35, Paris 1886, 910.

The Word Among Us publishes a monthly devotional magazine, books, Bible studies, and pamphlets that help Catholics grow in their faith.

To learn more about who we are and what we publish, visit www.wau.org. There you will find a variety of Catholic resources that will help you grow in your faith.

Your review makes a difference! If you enjoyed this book, please consider sharing your review on Amazon using the QR code below.

Embrace His Word
Listen to God . . .

www.wau.org

www.ingramcontent.com/pod-product-compliance
Lightning Source LLC
Chambersburg PA
CBHW070112080526
44586CB00013B/1273